Feasts

FEASTS

selected and edited by
CHRISTOPHER BLAND
and
LINDA KELLY

Constable · London

First published in Great Britain 1987
by Constable and Company Limited
10 Orange Street, London WC2H 7EG
Copyright © 1987 by Christopher Bland
and Linda Kelly
Set in Linotron Bembo 11pt by
Rowland Phototypesetting Limited
Bury St Edmunds, Suffolk
Printed in Great Britain by
St Edmundsbury Press Limited
Bury St Edmunds, Suffolk

British Library CIP data
Feasts.
1. Food–Literary collections
I. Bland, Christopher   II. Kelly, Linda
808.8'0355   PN 6071.F6

ISBN 0 09 467760 3

TO ARCHIE

Contents

Contents

Contents

Contents

Contents

Contents

TABLE D'HÔTE

Acknowledgements

We should like to make acknowledgement to the following for extracts used from their books:

The Estate of F. Scott Fitzgerald for F. Scott Fitzgerald's *The Great Gatsby*; Jonathan Cape Ltd and the Estate of James Joyce for James Joyce's *Ulysses* and *The Dubliners*; Glidrose Productions Ltd for Ian Fleming's *On Her Majesty's Secret Service*; the executors of the Ernest Hemingway Estate for Ernest Hemingway's *The First Forty-Nine Stories*; Mrs Laura Huxley and Chatto & Windus Ltd for Aldous Huxley's *Crome Yellow*; Chatto & Windus Ltd for Marcel Proust's *Remembrance of Things Past*, translated by C. K. Scott-Moncrieff and Terence Kilmartin; The Hogarth Press for Laurie Lee's *Cider with Rosie*; The Hogarth Press and the Estate of Virginia Woolf for Virginia Woolf's *Orlando* and *To The Lighthouse*; Collins Harvill for Giuseppe Tomasi di Lampedusa's *The Leopard*, translated by Archibald Colquhoun; Collins for T. H. White's *The Sword in the Stone*; Constable & Company Ltd for David Hughes's *The Pork Butcher* and Damon Runyon's *A Piece of Pie*; the Curtis Brown Group Ltd for W. H. Auden and Louis MacNeice's *Letters from Iceland* and for Stella Gibbons's *Cold Comfort Farm*; André Deutsch for John Updike's *Rabbit Redux*; Gerald Duckworth & Co Ltd for Hilaire Belloc's *Cautionary Verses*; Faber & Faber for Siegfried Sassoon's *Memoirs of a Fox-Hunting Man*, and for William Golding's *Lord of the Flies*; Hamish Hamilton for William Boyd's *Stars and Bars*, and for Truman Capote's *Breakfast at Tiffany's*; John Farquharson for Somerville and Ross's *The Further Experiences of an Irish R.M.*; Victor Gollancz Ltd for Kingsley Amis's *Lucky Jim*; John Hawkins & Associates Inc, New York for Harry Crews's *A Feast of Snakes*; the Estate of the late Sonia Brownell Orwell and Secker and Warburg Ltd for George Orwell's *Nineteen Eighty-Four*; William Heinemann Ltd for Anthony Burgess's *A Clockwork Orange*, and for John Steinbeck's *Cannery Row*; J. M. Dent for Dylan Thomas's *Under Milk Wood* and *The Collected Letters of Dylan Thomas*, edited by Paul Ferris; Macmillan & Co Ltd for Norman Mailer's *Ancient Evenings* and C. P. Snow's *The Masters*; McGraw-Hill Book Company for Vladimir Nabokov's *Ada*; John Murray (Publishers) Ltd for Patrick Leigh Fermor's *Mani*; Pan Books for Douglas Adams's *The Restaurant at the End of the Universe*; Michael Joseph Ltd for H. E. Bates's *Love for Lydia*; Michael Joseph and Penguin Books for Roald Dahl's *Someone Like You*; A. D. Peters & Co for C. S. Forester's *The Happy Return*, J. B. Priestley's *The Good Companions*, Evelyn Waugh's *Black Mischief*, and Nancy Mitford's *The Blessing*; Deborah Rogers for Stanley Crawford's *Gascoyne*; A. P. Watt Ltd on behalf of the Royal Literary Fund and William Heinemann Ltd for W. Somerset Maugham's *Complete Short Stories* and *The Collected Stories*; A. P. Watt Ltd on behalf of the Estate of K. S. P. McDowell and William Heinemann Ltd for E. F. Benson's *Queen Lucia*; A. P. Watt Ltd on behalf of the trustees of the Wodehouse Trust and Century Hutchinson for P. G. Wodehouse's *The Code of the Woosters* and *Carry on Jeeves*; A. P. Watt Ltd on behalf of the literary executors of the Estate of H. G. Wells for H. G. Wells's *Kipps*; Penguin Books Ltd for Emile Zola's *L'Assommoir*, translated by L. W. Tancock; Martin Secker and Warburg Ltd for Tom Sharpe's *Porterhouse Blue*; Unwin Hyman Ltd for J. R. R. Tolkien's *The Two Towers*; and The Bodley Head for Graham Greene's *Monsignor Quixote*. The picture on the jacket is reproduced by permission of The Bridgeman Art Library.

C. B.
L. K.
1987

Introduction

The theme of meals in literature – from Trimalchio's feast to the Mad Hatter's tea party – is one with endless variations. In this selection we have followed our own literary preferences and prejudices, concentrating mainly on writers of the nineteenth and twentieth centuries, with a few excursions into the classics: Virgil's table heaped with dainties, Cleopatra's pearl in vinegar, are irresistible inclusions.

Each meal is an event in the book in which it occurs. The subjects range from the purely festive to the romantic, the comic and the macabre. The Cratchits murmur with delight at 'a feathered phenomenon of a goose and a speckled cannon-ball of a Christmas pudding'; Tancredi is excited simultaneously by a towering, glistening, burnished gold macaroni pie – and by Angelica; the three fat women of Antibes abandon their diets and restore their friendship over croissants, pâté de foie gras, éclairs and double dry martinis; Basil Seal drinks toddy with the Azanian chiefs and eats his fiancée. Other meals might more properly be described as anti-feasts – few of us would relish snake steak supper (even when the half-inch pieces are soaked in vinegar, rolled in flour and fried), or the talkative Dish of the Day, encouraging diners to taste its rich and tender liver.

On many occasions the meal is a metaphor. We understand Anisya Fyodorovna's relationship with the uncle through her buttermilk biscuits, foaming mead and nuts preserved in honey. The rich hot smell of Inner Party coffee is an emanation from Winston's early childhood and a symbol of the forbidden. The costly, plain breakfast service, with bacon under silver covers and devilled kidneys frizzling on a hot water dish, describes the well-furnished, unostentatious lives of the inhabitants of Plumstead Episcopi rectory. Orlando calls his love a melon, a pineapple, an olive tree, an emerald and a fox in the snow, and does not know whether he has heard, seen or tasted the princess – or all three together. The inability of women in the South of England to bake a Yorkshire pudding, 'light as a feather, crisp and brarn, just a top and a bottom' expresses perfectly the Yorkshireman's age-old distrust of southern decadence. And James Bond's careful selection of Taittinger Blanc de Blanc, turbot poché, sauce mousseline, half a roast partridge, Mouton Rothschild '53 and ten-year-old Calvados demonstrates 007's belief that we are what we eat.

We have made some interesting discoveries in the course of our researches. The Mad Hatter's tea party, as we found out on re-reading, has no mention of food in it at all; as one of the most famous meals in literature we have included it nonetheless. The story of Cleopatra's pearl, dimly remembered from childhood, was finally tracked down, with the help of an erudite librarian, under the heading 'Oysters' in Pliny the Elder's *Natural History*. And the rumbustious tavern supper in *Tom Jones*, so clearly recalled by many, has no place in the novel of that name – a case of mistaking the film for the book. Our thanks to those who suggested it all the same, and for other more constructive ideas to the following: Melvyn Bragg, Sarah Bury, the Hon. James Byng, Lord Dacre, Ben Glazebrook, Caspar Hall, Xandra Hardie, Peter Jay, Nicholas Kelly, Princess Nina Lobanov, Simon McNair Scott, Eliza Pakenham and Tim Williams. The research has been entirely pleasurable; we hope the reading will be too. *Bon appetit!*

C.B.
L.K.
May, 1987

BREAKFASTS

Breakfast with Merlyn

'Now breakfast,' said Merlyn.

The Wart saw that the most perfect breakfast was laid out neatly for two, on a table before the window. There were peaches. There were also melons, strawberries and cream, rusks, brown trout piping hot, grilled perch which were much nicer, chicken devilled enough to burn one's mouth out, kidneys and mushrooms on toast, fricassee, curry, and a choice of boiling coffee or best chocolate made with cream in large cups.

'Have some mustard,' said the magician, when they had got to the kidneys.

The mustard-pot got up and walked over to his plate on thin silver legs that waddled like the owl's. Then it uncurled its handles and one handle lifted its lid with exaggerated courtesy while the other helped him to a generous spoonful.

'Oh, I love the mustard-pot!' cried the Wart. 'Wherever did you get it?'

At this the pot beamed all over its face and began to strut a bit, but Merlyn rapped it on the head with a teaspoon, so that it sat down and shut up at once.

'It is not a bad pot,' he said grudgingly. 'Only it is inclined to give itself airs.'

The Wart was so much impressed by the kindness of the old man, and particularly by the lovely things which he possessed, that he hardly liked to ask him personal questions. It seemed politer to sit still and to speak when he was spoken to. But Merlyn did not speak much, and when he did speak it was never in questions, so that the Wart had little opportunity for conversation. At last his curiosity got the better of him, and he asked something which had been puzzling him for some time.

'Would you mind if I ask you a question?'

'It is what I am for.'
'How did you know to set breakfast for two?'

T. H. White: *The Sword in the Stone*

Tufts of primroses

At this moment, a pretty serving-maid entered the room. She laid the dapper-cloth and arranged the table with a self-possession quite admirable. She seemed unconscious that any being was in the chamber except herself, or that there were any other duties to perform in life beyond filling a salt-cellar or folding a napkin.

'She does not even look at us,' said Coningsby when she had quitted the room, 'and I dare say only a prude.'

'She is calm,' said the stranger, 'because she is mistress of her subject; 'tis the secret of self-possession. She is here, as a duchess at court.'

They brought in Coningsby's meal, and he invited the stranger to join him. The invitation was accepted with cheerfulness.

''Tis but simple fare,' said Coningsby as the maiden uncovered the still hissing bacon and the eggs that looked like tufts of primroses.

'Nay, a national dish,' said the stranger, glancing quickly at the table, 'whose fame is a proverb. And what more should we expect under a simple roof! How much better than an omelette or a greasy olla, that they would give us in a posada! 'Tis a wonderful country this England! What a napkin! How spotless! And so sweet, I declare 'tis a perfume. There is not a princess throughout the South of Europe served with the cleanliness that meets us in this cottage.'

'An inheritance from our Saxon fathers?' said Coningsby. 'I apprehend the northern nations have a greater sense of cleanliness – of propriety – of what we call comfort?'

'By no means,' said the stranger, 'the East is the Land of the Bath. Moses and Mahomet made cleanliness religion.'

'You will let me help you?' said Coningsby, offering him a plate which he had filled.

'I thank you,' said the stranger, 'but it is one of my bread days.

With your permission this shall be my dish,' and he cut from the large loaf a supply of crusts.

'"Tis but unsavoury fare after a gallop,' said Coningsby.

'Ah! you are proud of your bacon and your eggs,' said the stranger smiling; 'but I love corn and wine. They are our chief and our oldest luxuries. Time has brought us substitutes, but how inferior; Man has deified corn and wine! but not even the Chinese or the Irish have raised temples to tea and potatoes.'

'But Ceres without Bacchus,' said Coningsby, 'how does that do? Think you, under this roof we could invoke the God?'

'Let us swear by his body that we will try,' said the stranger.

Alas! the landlord was not a priest of Bacchus. But then these inquiries led to the finest perry in the world. The young men agreed they had seldom tasted anything more delicious; they sent for another bottle. Coningsby, who was much interested by his new companion, enjoyed himself amazingly.

Benjamin Disraeli: *Coningsby*

At the Welches'

Breakfast technics at the Welches', like many of their ways of thought, recalled an earlier epoch. The food was kept hot on the sideboard in what Dixon conjectured were chafing-dishes. The quantity and variety of this food recalled in turn the fact that Mrs Welch supplemented Welch's professorial salary with a good-sized income of her own. Dixon had often wondered how Welch had contrived to marry money; it could hardly have been due to any personal merit, real or supposed, and the vagaries of Welch's mind could leave no room there for avarice. Perhaps the old fellow had had when younger what he now so demonstrably lacked: a way with him. In spite of the ravages wrought by his headache and his fury, Dixon felt happier as he wondered what foods would this morning afford visible proof of the Welches' prosperity. He went into the breakfast-room with the bed-clothes and Margaret a long way from the foreground of his mind.

The only person in the room was the Callaghan girl, sitting behind a well-filled plate. Dixon said good morning to her.

'Oh, good morning.' Her tone was neutral, not hostile.

He quickly decided on a bluff, speak-my-mind approach as the best cloak for rudeness, past or to come. One of his father's friends, a jeweller, had got away with conversing almost entirely in insults for the fifteen years Dixon had known him, merely by using this simple device. Deliberately intensifying his northern accent, Dixon said: 'Afraid I got off on the wrong foot with you last night.'

She looked up quickly, and he saw with bitterness how pretty her neck was. 'Oh . . . that. I shouldn't worry too much about it if I were you. I didn't show up too well myself.'

'Nice of you to take it like that,' he said, remembering that he'd already had one occasion to use this phrase to her. 'Very bad manners it was on my part, anyway.'

'Well, let's forget it, shall we?'

'Glad to; thanks very much.'

There was a pause, while he noted with mild surprise how much and how quickly she was eating. The remains of a large pool of sauce were to be seen on her plate beside a diminishing mound of fried egg, bacon, and tomatoes. Even as he watched she replenished her stock of sauce with a fat scarlet gout from the bottle. She glanced up and caught his look of interest, raised her eyebrows, and said, 'I'm sorry, I like sauce; I hope you don't mind,' but not convincingly, and he fancied she blushed.

'That's all right,' he said heartily; 'I'm fond of the stuff myself.' He pushed aside his bowl of cornflakes. They were of a kind he didn't like: malt had been used in their preparation. A study of the egg and bacon and tomatoes opposite him made him decide to postpone eating any himself. His gullet and stomach felt as if they were being deftly sewn up as he sat. He poured and drank a cup of black coffee, then refilled his cup.

'Aren't you going to have any of this stuff?' the girl asked.

'Well, not yet, I don't think.'

'What's the matter? Aren't you feeling so good?'

'No, not really, I must admit. Bit of a headache, you know.'

Kingsley Amis: *Lucky Jim*

Inner Party coffee

At this moment there was a quick step on the stairs. Julia burst into the room. She was carrying a tool-bag of coarse brown canvas, such as he had sometimes seen her carrying to and fro at the Ministry. He started forward to take her in his arms, but she disengaged herself rather hurriedly, partly because she was still holding the tool-bag.

'Half a second,' she said. 'Just let me show you what I've brought. Did you bring some of that filthy Victory Coffee? I thought you would. You can chuck it away again, because we shan't be needing it. Look here.'

She fell on her knees, threw open the bag, and tumbled out some spanners and a screwdriver that filled the top part of it. Underneath were a number of neat paper packets. The first packet that she passed to Winston had a strange and yet vaguely familiar feeling. It was filled with some kind of heavy, sand-like stuff which yielded wherever you touched it.

'It isn't sugar?' he said.

'Real sugar. Not saccharine, sugar. And here's a loaf of bread – proper white bread, not our bloody stuff – and a little pot of jam. And here's a tin of milk – but look! This is the one I'm really proud of. I had to wrap a bit of sacking round it, because –'

But she did not need to tell him why she had wrapped it up. The smell was already filling the room, a rich hot smell which seemed like an emanation from his early childhood, but which one did occasionally meet with even now, blowing down a passage-way before a door slammed, or diffusing itself mysteriously in a crowded street, sniffed for an instant and then lost again.

'It's coffee,' he murmured, 'real coffee.'

'It's Inner Party coffee. There's a whole kilo here,' she said.

'How did you manage to get hold of all these things?'

'It's all Inner Party stuff. There's nothing those swine don't have, nothing. But of course waiters and servants and people pinch things, and – look, I got a little packet of tea as well.'

Winston had squatted down beside her. He tore open a corner of the packet.

'It's real tea. Not blackberry leaves.'

'There's been a lot of tea about lately. They've captured India, or something,' she said vaguely. 'But listen, dear. I want you to turn your back on me for three minutes. Go and sit on the other side of the bed. Don't go too near the window. And don't turn round till I tell you.'

George Orwell: *Nineteen Eighty-Four*

Breakfast at St Ambrose College

Every morning the boy from the Weirs arrived with freshly caught gudgeon, and now and then an eel or trout, which the scouts on the staircase had learnt to fry delicately in oil. Fresh watercresses came in the same basket and the college kitchen furnished a spatchcocked chicken or grilled turkey's leg. In the season there were plover's eggs; or, at the worst, there was a dainty omelet; and a distant baker, famed for his light rolls and high charges, sent in the bread – the common domestic college loaf being of course out of the question for anyone with the slightest pretensions to taste and fit only for the perquisite of scouts. Then there would be a deep Yorkshire pie, or a reservoir of potted game, as a *pièce de résistance*, and three or four sorts of preserves, and a large cool tankard of cider cup or ale-cup to finish up with, or soda water and maraschino for a change. Tea and coffee were there indeed, but merely as a complement to those respectable beverages, for they were rarely touched by the breakfast-eaters of No 3 staircase.

Thomas Hughes: *Tom Brown at Oxford*

THE FOOD OF LOVE

Dinner at Donnafugata

The Prince was too experienced to offer Sicilian guests, in a town of the interior, a dinner beginning with soup, and he infringed the rules of *haute cuisine* all the more readily as he disliked it himself. But rumours of the barbaric foreign usage of serving an insipid liquid as first course had reached the citizens of Donnafugata too insistently for them not to quiver with a slight residue of alarm at the start of a solemn dinner like this. So when three lackeys in green, gold and powder entered, each holding a great silver dish containing a towering macaroni pie, only four of the twenty at table avoided showing pleased surprise; the Prince and Princess from fore-knowledge, Angelica from affectation and Concetta from lack of appetite. All the others (including Tancredi, I regret to say), showed their relief in varying ways, from the fluty and ecstatic grunts of the notary to the sharp squeak of Francesco Paolo. But a threatening circular stare from the host soon stifled these improper demonstrations.

Good manners apart, though, the aspect of those monumental dishes of macaroni was worthy of the quivers of admiration they evoked. The burnished gold of the crusts, the fragrance of sugar and cinnamon they exuded, were but preludes to the delights released from the interior when the knife broke the crust; first came a smoke laden with aromas, then chicken livers, hard boiled eggs, sliced ham, chicken and truffles in masses of piping hot, glistening macaroni, to which the meat juice gave an exquisite hue of suède.

The beginning of the meal, as happens in the provinces, was quiet. The arch-priest made the sign of the Cross and plunged in head first without a word. The organist absorbed the succulent dish with closed eyes; he was grateful to the Creator that his ability to shoot hare and woodcock could bring him ecstatic pleasures like this, and the thought came to him that he and Teresina could exist for a month on the cost of one of these dishes; Angelica, the lovely Angelica, forgot her Tuscan affectations and part of her good manners and devoured her food with the appetite of her seventeen years and the vigour given by grasping her fork half-way up the handle. Tancredi, in an attempt to link gallantry with greed, tried to imagine himself tasting, in the aromatic forkfuls, the kisses of his neighbour Angelica, but he realised at once that the experiment was disgusting and suspended it, with a mental reserve about reviving this fantasy with the pudding; the Prince, although rapt in the contemplation of Angelica sitting opposite him, was the only one at table able to notice that the *demi-glace* was overfilled, and made a mental note to tell the cook so next day; the others ate without thinking of anything, and without realising that the food seemed so delicious because sensuality was circulating in the house.

All were calm and contented. All except Concetta. She had of course embraced and kissed Angelica, told her not to use the formal third person and insisted on the familiar *tu* of their infancy, but under her pale blue bodice her heart was being torn to shreds; the violent Salina blood came surging up in her, and beneath a smooth forehead she found herself brooding over day-dreams of poisoning. Tancredi was sitting between her and Angelica and distributing, with the slightly forced air of one who feels in the wrong, his glances, compliments and jokes equally between both neighbours; but Concetta had an intuition, an animal intuition of the current of desire flowing from her cousin towards the intruder, and the little frown between her nose and forehead deepened; she wanted to kill as much as she wanted to die. But being a woman she snatched at details; Angelica's little finger in the air when her hand held her glass; a reddish mole on the skin of her neck; an attempt, half repressed, to remove with a finger a shred of food stuck in her very white teeth; she noticed even more sharply a certain coarseness of spirit; and to these details, which were really quite insignificant as they were cauterised by sensual fascination, she clung as trustingly and desperately as a falling builder's boy snatches at a leaden gutter; she hoped that Tancredi would notice too and be revolted by these obvious traces of ill-breeding. But Tancredi had already noticed them, and, alas! with no result. He was letting himself be drawn along by the physical stimulus of a beautiful woman to his fiery youth, and also by the (as-it-were) numerical excitement aroused by a rich girl in the mind of a man ambitious and poor.

At the end of dinner the conversation became general; Don Calogero told in bad Italian but with knowing insight some inside stories about the conquest of the province by Garibaldi; the notary told the Princess of a little house he was having built 'out of town'; Angelica, excited by light, food, Chablis and the obvious admiration she was arousing in every man around the table, asked Tancredi to describe some episodes of the 'glorious battle' for Palermo. She had put an elbow on the table and was leaning her cheek on her hand. Her face was flushed and she was perilously attractive to behold; the arabesque made by her forearm, elbow, finger and hanging white glove seemed exquisite to Tancredi and repulsive to Concetta. The young man, while continuing to admire, was describing the campaign as if it had all been quite light and unimportant; the night march on Gibilrossa, the scene between Bixio and La Masa, the assault on Porta di Termini. 'It was the greatest fun, signorina. Our biggest laugh was on the night of the 28th of May. The general needed a look-out post at the top of the convent at Origlione; we knocked, banged, cursed, knocked again: no one opened; it was an enclosed convent. Then Tassoni, Aldrighetti, I and one or two others tried to break down the door with our rifle butts. Nothing doing. We ran to fetch a beam from a shelled house nearby and finally, with a hellish din, the door gave way. We went in; not a soul in sight, but from a corner of the passage we heard desperate screams; a group of nuns had taken refuge in the chapel and were all crouching round the altar; I wonder *what* they feared at the hands of those dozen excited young men! They looked absurd, old and ugly in their black habits, with starting eyes, ready and prepared for . . . martyrdom. They were whining like bitches. Tassoni, who's a card, shouted: 'Nothing doing, sisters, we've other things to think of; but we'll be back when you've some novices.' And we all laughed fit to burst. Then we left them there, their tongues hanging out, to go and shoot at Royalists from the terraces above. Ten minutes later I was wounded.'

Angelica laughed, still leaning on her elbow, and showed all her pointed teeth. The joke seemed most piquant to her; that hint of rape perturbed her; her lovely throat quivered. 'What fine lads you must have been! How I wish I'd been with you!' Tancredi seemed transformed; the excitement of the story, the thrill of memory, mingling with the agitation produced by the girl's air of sensuality, changed him for an instant from the gentle youth he was in reality into a brutal and licentious soldier.

'Had you been there, signorina, we'd have had nò need to wait for novices.'

Angelica had heard a lot of coarse talk at home; but this was the first time (and not the last) when she found herself the object of a sexual double meaning; the novelty of it pleased her, her laughter went up a tone, became strident.

At that moment everyone rose from the table . . .

Giuseppe di Lampedusa: *The Leopard*
(translated by Archibald Colquhoun)

He called her a melon, a pineapple, an olive tree . . .

The person, whatever the name or sex, was about middle height, very slenderly fashioned, and dressed entirely in oyster-coloured velvet, trimmed with some unfamiliar greenish coloured fur. But these details were obscured by the extraordinary seductiveness which issued from the whole person. Images, metaphors of the most extreme and extravagant, twined and twisted in his mind. He called her a melon, a pineapple, an olive tree, an emerald, and a fox in the snow all in the space of three seconds; he did not know whether he had heard her, tasted her, seen her, or all three together. (For though we must pause not a moment in the narrative we may here hastily note that all his images at this time were simple in the extreme to match his senses and were mostly taken from things he had liked the taste of as a boy. But if his senses were simple they were at the same time extremely strong. To pause therefore and seek the reason of things is out of the question.) . . . A melon, an emerald, a fox in the snow – so he raved, so he stared. When the boy, for alas, a boy it must be – no woman could skate with such speed and vigour – swept almost on tiptoe past him, Orlando was ready to tear his hair with vexation that the person was of his own sex, and thus all embraces were out of the question. But the skater came closer. Legs, hands, carriage, were a boy's, but no boy ever had a mouth like that; no boy had those breasts; no boy had eyes which looked as if they had been fished from the bottom of the sea. Finally, coming to a stop and sweeping a curtsey with the utmost grace to the King, who was shuffling past on the arm of some Lord-in-waiting, the unknown skater came to a standstill. She was not a handsbreadth off. She was a woman. Orlando stared; trembled; turned hot; turned cold; longed to hurl himself through the summer air; to crush acorns beneath his feet; to toss his arms with the beech trees and the oaks. As it was, he drew his lips up over his small white teeth; opened them perhaps half an inch as if to bite; shut them as if he had bitten. The Lady Euphrosyne hung upon his arm.

The stranger's name, he found, was the Princess Marousha Stanilovska Dagmar Natasha Iliana Romanovitch, and she had come in the train of the Muscovite Ambassador, who was her uncle perhaps, or perhaps her father, to attend the coronation. Very little was known of the Muscovites. In their great beards and furred hats they sat almost silent; drinking some black liquid which they spat out now and then upon the ice. None spoke English, and French with which some at least were familiar was then little spoken at the English Court.

It was through this accident that Orlando and the Princess became acquainted. They were seated opposite each other at the great table spread under a huge awning for the entertainment of the notables. The Princess was placed between two young Lords, one Lord Francis Vere and the other the young Earl of Moray. It was laughable to see the predicament she soon had them in, for though both were fine lads in their way, the babe unborn had as much knowledge of the French tongue as they had. When at the beginning of dinner the Princess turned to the Earl and said, with a grace which ravished his heart, '*Je crois avoir fait la connaissance d'un gentilhomme qui vous était apparenté en Pologne l'été dernier,*' or '*La beauté des dames de la cour d'Angleterre me met dans le ravissement. On ne peut voir une dame plus gracieuse que votre reine, ni une coiffure plus belle que la sienne,*' both Lord Francis and the Earl showed the highest embarrassment. The one helped her largely to horse-radish sauce, the other whistled to his dog and made him beg for a marrow-bone. At this the Princess could no longer contain her laughter, and Orlando, catching her eyes across the boars' heads and stuffed peacocks, laughed too. He laughed, but the laugh on his lips froze in wonder. Whom had he loved, what had he loved, he asked himself in a tumult of emotion, until now? An old woman, he answered, all skin and bone. Red-cheeked trulls too many to mention. A puling nun. A hard-bitten, cruel-mouthed adventuress. A nodding mass of lace and ceremony. Love had meant to him nothing but sawdust and cinders. The joys he had had of it tasted insipid in the extreme. He marvelled how he could have gone through with it without yawning. For as he looked the thickness of his blood melted; the ice turned to wine in his veins; he heard the waters flowing and the birds singing; spring broke over the hard wintry landscape; his manhood woke; he grasped a sword in his hand; he charged a more daring foe than Pole or Moor; he dived in deep water; he saw the flower of danger growing in a crevice; he stretched his hand – in fact he was rattling off one of his most impassioned sonnets when the Princess addressed him, 'Would you have the goodness to pass the salt?'

He blushed deeply.

'With all the pleasure in the world, Madame,' he replied, speaking French with a perfect accent. For, heaven be praised, he spoke the tongue as his own; his mother's maid had taught him. Yet perhaps it would have been better for him had he never learnt that tongue; never answered that voice; never followed the light of those eyes . . .

The Princess continued. Who were those bumpkins, she asked him, who sat beside her with the manners of stablemen? What was the nauseating mixture they had poured on her plate? Did the dogs eat at the same table with the men in England? Was that figure of fun at the end of the table with her hair rigged up like a Maypole (*comme une grande perche mal fagotée*) really the Queen? And did the King always slobber like that? And which of those popinjays was George Villiers? Though these questions rather discomposed Orlando at first, they were put with such archness and drollery that he could not help but laugh; and as he saw from the blank faces of the company that nobody understood a word, he answered her as freely as she asked him, speaking, as he did, in perfect French.

Thus began an intimacy between the two which soon became the scandal of the Court.

Virginia Woolf: *Orlando*

Becky sets her cap at Joseph

Downstairs, then, they went, Joseph very red and blushing, Rebecca very modest, and holding her green eyes downwards. She was dressed in white, with bare shoulders as white as snow – the picture of youth, unprotected innocence, and humble virgin simplicity. 'I must be very quiet,' thought Rebecca, 'and very much interested about India.'

Now we have heard how Mrs Sedley had prepared a fine curry for her son, just as he liked it, and in the course of dinner a portion of this dish was offered to Rebecca. 'What is it?' said she, turning an appealing look to Mr Joseph.

'Capital,' said he. His mouth was full of it; his face quite red with the delightful exercise of gobbling. 'Mother, it's as good as my own curries in India.'

'Oh, I must try some, if it is an Indian dish,' said Miss Rebecca. 'I am sure everything must be good that comes from there.'

'Give Miss Sharp some curry, my dear,' said Mr Sedley, laughing.

Rebecca had never tasted the dish before.

'Do you find it as good as everything else from India?' said Mr Sedley.

'Oh, excellent!' said Rebecca, who was suffering tortures with the cayenne pepper.

'Try a chili with it, Miss Sharp,' said Joseph, really interested.

'A chili,' said Rebecca, gasping. 'O yes!' She thought a chili was something cool, as its name imported, and was served with some. 'How fresh and green they look!' she said, and put one into her mouth. It was hotter than the curry; flesh and blood could bear it no longer. She laid down her fork. 'Water, for Heaven's sake, water!' she cried. Mr Sedley burst out laughing (he was a coarse man, from the Stock Exchange, where they love all sorts of practical jokes). 'They are real Indian, I assure you,' said he. 'Sambo, give Miss Sharp some water.'

The paternal laugh was echoed by Joseph, who thought the joke capital. The ladies only smiled a little. They thought poor Rebecca suffered too much. She would have liked to choke old Sedley, but she swallowed her mortification as well as she had the abominable curry before it, and as soon as she could speak, said, with a comical, good-humoured air –

'I ought to have remembered the pepper which the Princess of Persia puts in the cream-tarts in the *Arabian Nights*. Do you put cayenne into your cream-tarts in India, sir?'

Old Sedley began to laugh, and thought Rebecca was a good-humoured girl. Joseph simply said – 'Cream-tarts, Miss? Our cream is very bad in Bengal. We generally use goats' milk; and, 'gad, do you know, I've got to prefer it!'

'You won't like *everything* from India now, Miss Sharp,' said the old gentleman; but when the ladies had retired after dinner, the wily old fellow said to his son, 'Have a care, Joe; that girl is setting her cap at you.'

W. M. Thackeray: *Vanity Fair*

After the ride

The day was darkening; a beaming vestige of sunlight lingered in a western strip of the overcast sky: we have all seen the person who after gaily greeting a friend crosses the street with that smile still fresh on his face – to be eclipsed by the stare of the stranger who might have missed the cause and mistaken the effect for the bright leer of madness. Having worked out that metaphor, Van and Ada decided it was really time to go home. As they rode through Gamlet, the sight of a Russian *traktir* gave such a prod to their hunger that they dismounted and entered the dim little tavern. A coachman drinking tea from the saucer, holding it up to his loud lips in his large claw, came straight from a pretzel-string of old novels. There was nobody else in the steamy hole save a kerchiefed woman pleading with (*ugovarivayushchaya*) a leg-dangling lad in a red shirt to get on with his fish soup. She proved to be the *traktir*-keeper and rose, 'wiping her hands on her apron', to bring Ada (whom she recognized at once) and Van (whom she supposed, not incorrectly, to be the little chatelaine's 'young man') some small Russian-type 'hamburgers' called *bitochki*. Each devoured half a dozen of them – then they retrieved their bikes from under the jasmins to pedal on. They had to light their carbide lamps. They made a last pause before reaching the darkness of Ardis Park.

By a kind of lyrical coincidence they found Marina and Mlle Larivière having evening tea in the seldom-used Russian-style glassed-in veranda. The novelist, who was now quite restored, but still in flowery négligé, had just finished reading her new story in its first fair copy (to be typed on the morrow) to Tokay-sipping Marina, who had *le vin triste* and was much affected by the suicide of the gentleman *'au cou rouge et puissant de veuf encore plein de sève'* who, frightened by his victim's fright, so to speak, had compressed too hard the throat of the little girl he had raped in a moment of *'gloutonnerie impardonnable'*.

Van drank a glass of milk and suddenly felt such a wave of delicious exhaustion invading his limbs that he thought he'd go straight to bed. '*Tant pis*,' said Ada, reaching voraciously for the *keks* (English fruit cake). 'Hammock?' she inquired; but tottering Van shook his head, and having kissed Marina's melancholy hand, retired.

'*Tant pis*,' repeated Ada, and with invincible appetite started to smear butter all over the yolk-tinted rough surface and rich incrustations – raisins, angelica, candied cherry, cedrat – of a thick slice of cake.

Mlle Larivière, who was following Ada's movements with awe and disgust, said:

'*Je rêve. Il n'est pas possible qu'on mette du beurre par-dessus toute cette pâte britannique, masse indigeste et immonde.*'

'*Et ce n'est que la première tranche,*' said Ada.

'Do you want a sprinkle of cinnamon on your *lait caillé*?' asked Marina. 'You know, Belle' (turning to Mlle Larivière), 'she used to call it "sanded snow" when she was a baby.'

'She was never a baby,' said Belle emphatically. 'She could break the back of her pony before she could walk.'

'I wonder,' asked Marina, 'how many miles you rode to have our athlete drained so thoroughly.'

'Only seven,' replied Ada with a munch smile.

Vladimir Nabokov: *Ada*

Understanding the uncle

Soon the door was opened obviously, from the sound, by a barefoot servant-girl, and a stout, red-cheeked, handsome woman of about forty, with a double chin and full red lips, walked in, with a big tray in her hands. With hospitable dignity and cordiality in her eyes and in every gesture, she looked round at the guests, and with a genial smile bowed to them respectfully.

In spite of her exceptional stoutness, which made her hold her head flung back, while her bosom and all her portly person was thrust forward, this woman (the uncle's housekeeper) stepped with extreme lightness. She went to the table, put the tray down, and deftly with her plump, white hands set the bottles and dishes on the table. When she had finished this task she went away, standing for a moment in the doorway with a smile on her face. 'Here I am – I am *she*! Now do you understand the uncle?' her appearance had said to Rostov. Who could fail to understand? Not Nikolay only, but even Natasha understood the uncle now and the significance of his knitted brows, and the happy, complacent smile, which puckered his lips as Anisya Fyodorovna came in. On the tray there were liqueurs, herb-brandy, mushrooms, biscuits of rye flour made with buttermilk, honey in the comb, foaming mead made from honey, apples, nuts raw and nuts baked, and nuts preserved in honey. Then Anisya Fyodorovna brought in preserves made with honey and with sugar, and ham and a chicken that had just been roasted.

All these delicacies were of Anisya Fyodorovna's preparing, cooking or preserving. All seemed to smell and taste, as it were, of Anisya Fyodorovna. All seemed to recall her buxomness, cleanliness, whiteness, and cordial smile.

'A little of this, please, little countess,' she kept saying, as she handed Natasha first one thing, then another. Natasha ate of everything, and it seemed to her that such buttermilk biscuits, such delicious preserves, such nuts in honey, such a chicken, she had never seen nor tasted anywhere. Anisya Fyodorovna withdrew. Rostov and the uncle, as they sipped cherry brandy after supper, talked of hunts past and to come, of Rugay, and Ilagin's dogs. Natasha sat upright on the sofa, listening with sparkling eyes. She tried several times to waken Petya, and make him eat something, but he made incoherent replies, evidently in his sleep. Natasha felt so gay, so well content in these new surroundings, that her only fear was that the trap would come too soon for her. After a silence had chanced to fall upon them, as almost always happens when any one receives friends for the first time in his own house, the uncle said, in response to the thought in his guests' minds:

'Yes, so you see how I am finishing my days . . . One dies – forward, quick march! – nothing is left. So why sin!'

Leo Tolstoy: *War and Peace*

Eugénie gives her cousin lunch

After two hours of busy occupation, in the course of which Eugénie left her work twenty times at least to go and watch the coffee boiling, or listen for sounds from her cousin's room announcing that he was getting up, she had succeeded in preparing a very simple, very inexpensive lunch, but one which was a terrible infringement of the immemorial customs and practice of the household. Midday lunch was a meal that no one thought of sitting down to table for. It consisted only of a little bread, some fruit or butter, and a glass of wine. Now as she looked at the table placed beside the fire, with one of the arm-chairs set before the place laid for her cousin, at the two plates of fruit, the egg-cups, the bottle of white wine, the bread, the sugar heaped up in a saucer, Eugénie trembled in every limb even to think of the stare her father would give her if he happened to come in at that moment. And so she kept looking at the clock to estimate if her cousin had time to finish lunch before the master of the house returned.

'Never mind, Eugénie. If your father comes in, I shall take the responsibility of doing all this on myself,' said Madame Grandet.

Eugénie could not keep back her tears. 'Oh! my darling mother,' she exclaimed, 'I have never loved you half enough!'

37

Charles, after strolling interminably about his room, humming and singing snatches of song to himself, came downstairs at last. Happily, it was still only eleven o'clock. True Parisian that he was, Charles had taken as much pains with his appearance as if he had been staying in the château of the noble lady who was travelling in Scotland. He came in with that affable laughing air that sits so well on a young man, and that made Eugénie rejoice and feel sorry for him in the same instant. He had taken the catastrophic collapse of his castles in Anjou as a joke, and greeted his aunt very gaily.

'Did you sleep well, my dear aunt? And you, too, cousin?'

'Yes, thank you. How did you sleep?' said Madame Grandet.

'Oh, I slept soundly.'

'You must be hungry, cousin,' said Eugénie. 'Sit down and have something to eat.'

'Oh, I never take breakfast before twelve o'clock, just after I get up. Still, I fared so badly on the way here that I'll place myself in your hands. Besides . . .' He drew out the most charming little flat watch that Bréguet ever made. 'Why, it's only eleven o'clock. I was up early this morning.'

'Up early? . . .' said Madame Grandet.

'Yes, but I wanted to put my things in order. Well, I am quite ready for something, anything will do, a bird, a partridge . . .'

'Holy Virgin!' cried Nanon, as she heard this.

'A partridge,' said Eugénie to herself, wishing she could lay out all she had to buy a partridge.

The dandy sank gracefully into the armchair, like a pretty woman reclining on a divan. Eugénie and her mother drew their chairs forward and sat near him, by the fire.

'Do you always live here?' Charles inquired, finding the room even more hideous by daylight than it had seemed by candlelight the evening before.

'Always,' Eugénie answered, with her eyes on him, 'except during the vintage. We go to help Nanon then, and we all stay at the Abbey at Noyers.'

'You never take a walk?'

'Sometimes on Sunday after vespers, when it is fine, we walk as far as the bridge,' said Madame Grandet; 'or in the hay-making season we go to watch the hay being cut.'

'Have you a theatre here?'

'Go to the play!' exclaimed Madame Grandet. 'Go to see play-actors! But do you not know that that's a mortal sin?'

'Here, sir,' said Nanon, bringing in the eggs, 'we are giving you chickens in the shell.'

'Oh, new-laid eggs!' said Charles, who, after the manner of people who take luxury for granted, had not given another thought to his partridge. 'How delicious! Now, what about a little butter, eh, my good girl?'

'Butter now? That means no cake later on!' said the servant.

'But of course bring some butter, Nanon!' cried Eugénie.

The girl watched her cousin cutting his bread and butter into strips to dip into his egg, and was as happy in the sight as the most romantic shop-girl in Paris watching the triumph of innocence in a melodrama. It is true that Charles, who had been brought up by a gracious, charming mother, and polished by an accomplished woman of the world, was as dainty, elegant, neat in his ways as any little milliner. The compassion and tenderness of a young girl have a truly magnetic force, and Charles, seeing himself thus waited upon by his cousin and aunt, could not help yielding without a struggle to the influence of the overwhelming current of feeling, that was, as it were, brought to bear upon him. He cast a glance at Eugénie of radiant good humour, a caressing glance that held a smile. As he looked at her he noticed the exquisite harmony of line of the features in her pure face, her innocent attitude of attention to him, the magical clearness of her eyes, alight with young dreams of love but with no heaviness of passion.

'Upon my word, my dear cousin, if you were in a box at the Opéra, and dressed in full fig, my aunt would be quite right to think of deadly sin, for all the men would be envious and all the women jealous.'

This compliment made Eugénie's heart stop beating, and then beat fast with delight, although it did not convey much meaning to her mind.

'Oh, you're making fun of your little country cousin!' she said.

'If you knew me better, cousin, you would know that I detest mockery: it hardens the heart, deadens all the feelings . . .' And he swallowed a strip of bread and butter with a very pleasant satisfaction.

'No, I never make fun of other people,' he went on, 'very probably because I haven't a keen enough wit, and I find this failing is a great disadvantage to me. In Paris they have a way of wiping a man out by saying, 'He's so good-natured!' By which they mean, 'The poor youth hasn't a spark – he's as dense as a rhinoceros.' But as I am well off and known to bring down my bird first shot at thirty paces, with any kind of pistol, anywhere, they don't poke fun at me.'

'What you say, nephew, shows that you have a kind heart.'

'You have a very pretty ring on your finger,' said Eugénie. 'Is it rude to ask if I may look at it?'

Charles held out his hand, pulling off his ring as he did so, and Eugénie blushed as the tips of her fingers touched her cousin's pink finger-nails.

'Look, mother, what fine workmanship!'

'There's a big lot of gold in that,' said Nanon, bringing in the coffee.

'What's that?' asked Charles, laughing. And he pointed to an oval pot of glazed brown earthenware, decorated outside with a border of cinders, in which the coffee grounds rose to the surface and fell again in the boiling liquid.

'It's piping hot coffee,' said Nanon.

'Oh, my dear aunt! I'll leave at least some useful remembrance of my stay here. You are very much behind the times! I will teach you how to make good coffee in a Chaptal coffee-pot.' And he endeavoured to explain the principle on which the Chaptal coffee-pot works.

'Well, bless me, if there's all that fuss about it you would have to spend all your time at it,' said Nanon. 'I'll never make coffee that way. No, indeed. And who would get grass for our cow while I was making the coffee?'

'I'll make it,' said Eugénie.

'My dear child!' said Madame Grandet, looking at her daughter.

At this, as they recalled the blow about to fall to overwhelm this unfortunate young man in misery, the three women fell silent and looked at him with an air of commiseration which caught his attention.

'What's the matter, cousin?' he asked.

'Hush!' said Madame Grandet, as Eugénie was going to answer. 'You know that your father means to speak to Monsieur –'

'Say "Charles",' said the young man.

'Oh, is your name Charles? What a nice name!' exclaimed Eugénie.

Dreaded misfortunes are nearly always sure to happen. Just at that moment Nanon, Madame Grandet, and Eugénie, who could not think of the old cooper's return without a shudder, heard a well-known knock echo through the house.

'That's Papa!' said Eugénie.

She swept away the saucer with the sugar, leaving a few lumps on the tablecloth. Nanon carried off the plate with the eggshells. Madame Grandet started up like a frightened deer. It was a scene of utter panic, to Charles's bewilderment and wonder.

'Why, what's the matter?' he asked.

'My father's here,' said Eugénie.

'But what of it? . . .'

Monsieur Grandet came into the room, cast one piercing glance at the table, at Charles, saw everything.

'Aha! You've been treating your nephew to a banquet, I see. That's good, very good, excellent indeed!' he said, without any hesitation in his speech. 'When the cat is away, the mice may play.'

'A banquet? . . .' Charles repeated to himself, quite unable to form any idea of the normal diet and customs of this household.

'Bring me my glass, Nanon,' said the winegrower.

Eugénie brought the glass. Grandet drew a large horn-handled clasp-knife from his pocket, cut a slice of bread, took a little butter and spread it carefully, and began to eat without sitting down. Charles was putting sugar into his coffee. Grandet noticed the lumps of sugar on the table-cloth; he looked narrowly at his wife, who turned pale and started backwards. He bent over to whisper in the poor old woman's ear:

'Where did you get all that sugar from?'

'Nanon went to Fessard's for some: we had none in the house.'

No one can imagine the painful interest that this tableau held for the three women. Nanon had left her kitchen and stood looking into the room to see how things were going there. Meanwhile Charles had tasted his coffee, and finding it rather strong was looking round the table for the sugar, which Grandet had already put away.

'What do you want, nephew?' the old man inquired.

'The sugar.'

'Put some more milk in,' said the master of the house, 'and your coffee will taste sweeter.'

Eugénie took up the saucer full of sugar, which Grandet had previously taken possession of, and replaced it on the table, looking her father calmly in the face as she did so. Certainly no Parisian lady, helping her lover to escape by holding the weight of his silk rope ladder with her weak arms, shows greater courage than Eugénie showed then, in putting the sugar back on the table. The Parisian will have her reward when she proudly displays to her lover a beautiful arm covered with bruises; each bruise will be kissed and bathed in tears, and pain forgotten in pleasure: while Charles would never have the remotest conception of the deadly terror that shook his cousin's heart, while she stood there stricken by the lightning of the old cooper's look.

Honoré de Balzac: *Eugénie Grandet*

June's treat

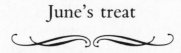

Dinner began in silence; the women facing one another, and the men.

In silence the soup was finished – excellent, if a little thick – and fish was brought. In silence it was handed.

Bosinney ventured: 'It's the first spring day.'

Irene echoed softly: 'Yes – the first spring day.'

'Spring!' said June: 'there isn't a breath of air!' No one replied.

The fish was taken away, a fine fresh sole from Dover. And Bilson brought champagne, a bottle swathed around the neck with white.

Soames said: 'You'll find it dry.'

Cutlets were handed, each pink-frilled about the legs. They were refused by June, and silence fell.

Soames said: 'You'd better take a cutlet, June; there's nothing coming.'

But June again refused, so they were borne away. And then Irene asked: 'Phil, have you heard my blackbird?'

Bosinney answered: 'Rather – he's got a hunting-song. As I came round I heard him in the Square.'

'He's such a darling!'

'Salad, sir?' Spring chicken was removed.

But Soames was speaking: 'The asparagus is very poor. Bosinney, glass of sherry with your sweet? June, you're drinking nothing!'

June said: 'You know I never do. Wine's such horrid stuff!'

An apple charlotte came upon a silver dish. And smilingly Irene said: 'The azaleas are so wonderful this year!'

To this Bosinney murmured: 'Wonderful! The scent's extraordinary!'

June said: 'How *can* you like the scent? Sugar, please, Bilson.'

Sugar was handed her, and Soames remarked: 'This charlotte's good!'

The charlotte was removed. Long silence followed. Irene, beckoning, said: 'Take out the azaleas, Bilson. Miss June can't bear the scent.'

'No, let it stay,' said June.

Olives from France, with Russian caviare, were placed on little plates. And Soames remarked: 'Why can't we have the Spanish?' But no one answered.

The olives were removed. Lifting her tumbler June demanded: 'Give me some water, please.' Water was given her. A silver tray was brought, with German plums. There was a lengthy pause. In perfect harmony all were eating them.

Bosinney counted up the stones: 'This year – next year – some time –'

Irene finished softly: 'Never. There was such a glorious sunset. The sky's all ruby still – so beautiful!'

He answered: 'Underneath the dark.'

Their eyes had met, and June cried scornfully: 'A London sunset!'

Egyptian cigarettes were handed in a silver box. Soames, taking one, remarked: 'What time's your play begin?'

No one replied, and Turkish coffee followed in enamelled cups.

Irene, smiling quietly, said: 'If only –'

'Only what?' said June.

'If only it could always be the spring!'

Brandy was handed; it was pale and old.

Soames said: 'Bosinney, better take some brandy.'

Bosinney took a glass; they all arose.

'You want a cab?' asked Soames.

June answered: 'No. My cloak, please, Bilson.' Her cloak was brought.

Irene, from the window, murmured: 'Such a lovely night! The stars are coming out!'

Soames added: 'Well, I hope you'll both enjoy yourselves.'

From the door June answered: 'Thanks. Come, Phil.'

Bosinney cried: 'I'm coming.'

Soames smiled a sneering smile, and said: 'I wish you luck!'

And at the door Irene watched them go.

Bosinney called: 'Good night!'

'Good night!' she answered softly . . .

John Galsworthy: *The Man of Property*

MURDER ON THE MENU

Death from the deep freeze

Later, one of the detectives came up and sat beside her. Did she know, he asked, of anything in the house that could've been used as the weapon? Would she mind having a look around to see if anything was missing – a very big spanner, for example, or a heavy metal vase.

They didn't have any heavy metal vases, she said.

'Or a big spanner?'

She didn't think they had a big spanner. But there might be some things like that in the garage.

The search went on. She knew that there were other policemen in the garden all around the house. She could hear their footsteps on the gravel outside, and sometimes she saw the flash of a torch through a chink in the curtains. It began to get late, nearly nine she noticed by the clock on the mantel. The four men searching the rooms seemed to be growing weary, a trifle exasperated.

'Jack,' she said, the next time Sergeant Noonan went by. 'Would you mind giving me a drink?'

'Sure I'll give you a drink. You mean this whisky?'

'Yes, please. But just a small one. It might make me feel better.'

He handed her the glass.

'Why don't you have one yourself,' she said. 'You must be awfully tired. Please do. You've been very good to me.'

'Well,' he answered. 'It's not strictly allowed, but I might take just a drop to keep me going.'

One by one the others came in and were persuaded to take a little nip of whisky. They stood around rather awkwardly with the drinks in their hands, uncomfortable in her presence, trying to say consoling things to her. Sergeant Noonan wandered into the kitchen, came out quickly and said, 'Look, Mrs Maloney. You know that oven of yours is still on, and the meat still inside.'

'Oh *dear* me!' she cried. 'So it is!'

'I better turn it off for you, hadn't I?'

'Will you do that, Jack. Thank you so much.'

When the sergeant returned the second time, she looked at him with her large, dark, tearful eyes. 'Jack Noonan,' she said.

'Yes?'

'Would you do me a small favour – you and these others?'

'We can try, Mrs Maloney.'

'Well,' she said. 'Here you all are, and good friends of dear Patrick's too, and helping to catch the man who killed him. You must be terrible hungry by now because it's long past your supper time, and I know Patrick would never forgive me, God bless his soul, if I allowed you to remain in his house without offering you decent hospitality. Why don't you eat up that lamb that's in the oven? It'll be cooked just right by now.'

'Wouldn't dream of it,' Sergeant Noonan said.

'Please,' she begged. 'Please eat it. Personally I couldn't touch a thing, certainly not what's been in the house when he was here. But it's all right for you. It'd be a favour to me if you'd eat it up. Then you can go on with your work again afterwards.'

There was a good deal of hesitating among the four policemen, but they were clearly hungry, and in the end they were persuaded to go into the kitchen and help themselves. The woman stayed where she was, listening to them through the open door, and she could hear them speaking among themselves, their voices thick and sloppy because their mouths were full of meat.

'Have some more, Charlie?'

'No. Better not finish it.'

'She *wants* us to finish it. She said so. Be doing her a favour.'

'Okay then. Give me some more.'

'That's the hell of a big club the guy must've used to hit poor Patrick,' one of them was saying. 'The doc says his skull was smashed all to pieces just like from a sledge-hammer.'

'That's why it ought to be easy to find.'

'Exactly what I say.'

'Whoever done it, they're not going to be carrying a thing like that around with them longer than they need.'

One of them belched.

'Personally, I think it's right here on the premises.'

'Probably right under our very noses. What you think, Jack?'
And in the other room, Mary Maloney began to giggle.

Roald Dahl: *Lamb for the Slaughter*

Cottage pie

FIRST VOICE

In the blind-drawn dark dining-room of School
House, dusty and echoing as a dining-room in a vault,
Mr and Mrs Pugh are silent over cold grey cottage pie.
Mr Pugh reads, as he forks the shroud meat in, from
Lives of the Great Poisoners. He has bound a plain
brown-paper cover round the book. Slyly, between
slow mouthfuls, he sidespies up at Mrs Pugh, poisons
her with his eye, then goes on reading. He underlines
certain passages and smiles in secret.

MRS PUGH

Persons with manners do not read at table,

FIRST VOICE

says Mrs Pugh. She swallows a digestive tablet as big
as a horse-pill, washing it down with clouded peasoup
water.

[*Pause*

MRS PUGH

Some persons were brought up in pigsties.

MR PUGH

Pigs don't read at table, dear.

FIRST VOICE

Bitterly she flicks dust from the broken cruet. It
settles on the pie in a thin gnat-rain.

MR PUGH

Pigs can't read, my dear.

MRS PUGH

I know one who can.

FIRST VOICE

Alone in the hissing laboratory of his wishes, Mr
Pugh minces among bad vats and jeroboams, tiptoes
through spinneys of murdering herbs, agony dancing
in his crucibles, and mixes especially for Mrs Pugh a
venomous porridge unknown to toxicologists which
will scald and viper through her until her ears fall
off like figs, her toes grow big and black as balloons,
and steam comes screaming out of her navel.

MR PUGH

You know best, dear,

FIRST VOICE

says Mr Pugh, and quick as a flash he ducks her in
rat soup.

MRS PUGH

What's that book by your trough, Mr Pugh?

MR PUGH

It's a theological work, my dear. *Lives of the Great
Saints.*

FIRST VOICE

Mrs Pugh smiles. An icicle forms in the cold air of
the dining-vault.

Dylan Thomas: *Under Milk Wood*

Canetons à la mode d'Amblève

A strange stillness hung over the restaurant; it was one of those rare
moments when the orchestra was not discoursing the strains of the
Ice-cream Sailor waltz.

'Did I ever tell you,' asked Clovis of his friend, 'the tragedy of
music at mealtimes?

Murder on the Menu

'It was a gala evening at the Grand Sybaris Hotel, and a special dinner was being served in the Amethyst dining-hall. The Amethyst dining-hall had almost a European reputation, especially with that section of Europe which is historically identified with the Jordan Valley. Its cooking was beyond reproach, and its orchestra was sufficiently highly salaried to be above criticism. Thither came in shoals the intensely musical and the almost intensely musical, who are very many, and in still greater numbers the merely musical, who know how Tschaikowsky's name is pronounced and can recognise several of Chopin's nocturnes if you give them due warning; these eat in the nervous, detached manner of roebuck feeding in the open, and keep anxious ears cocked towards the orchestra for the first hint of a recognisable melody.

'"Ah, yes, Pagliacci," they murmur, as the opening strains follow hot upon the soup, and if no contradiction is forthcoming from any better-informed quarter they break forth into subdued humming by way of supplementing the efforts of the musicians. Sometimes the melody starts on level terms with the soup, in which case the banqueters contrive somehow to hum between the spoonfuls; the facial expression of enthusiasts who are punctuating potage St Germain with Pagliacci is not beautiful, but it should be seen by those who are bent on observing all sides of life. One cannot discount the unpleasant things of this world merely by looking the other way.

'In addition to the aforementioned types the restaurant was patronised by a fair sprinkling of the absolutely non-musical; their presence in the dining-hall could only be explained on the supposition that they had come there to dine.

'The earlier stages of the dinner had worn off. The wine lists had been consulted, by some with the blank embarrassment of a schoolboy suddenly called on to locate a Minor Prophet in the tangled hinterland of the Old Testament, by others with the severe scrutiny which suggests that they have visited most of the higher-priced wines in their own homes and probed their family weaknesses. The diners who chose their wine in the latter fashion always gave their orders in a penetrating voice, with a plentiful garnishing of stage directions. By insisting on having your bottle pointing to the north when the cork is being drawn, and calling the waiter Max, you may induce an impression on your guests which hours of laboured boasting might

51

be powerless to achieve. For this purpose, however, the guests must be chosen as carefully as the wine.

'Standing aside from the revellers in the shadow of a massive pillar was an interested spectator who was assuredly of the feast, and yet not in it. Monsieur Aristide Saucourt was the *chef* of the Grand Sybaris Hotel, and if he had an equal in his profession he had never acknowledged the fact. In his own domain he was a potentate, hedged around with the cold brutality that Genius expects rather than excuses in her children; he never forgave, and those who served him were careful that there should be little to forgive. In the outer world, the world which devoured his creations, he was an influence; how profound or how shallow an influence he never attempted to guess. It is the penalty and the safeguard of genius that it computes itself by troy weight in a world that measures by vulgar hundredweights.

'Once in a way the great man would be seized with a desire to watch the effect of his master-efforts, just as the guiding brain of Krupp's might wish at a supreme moment to intrude into the firing line of an artillery duel. And such an occasion was the present. For the first time in the history of the Grand Hotel, he was presenting to its guests the dish which he had brought to that pitch of perfection which almost amounts to scandal. Canetons à la mode d'Amblève. In thin gilt lettering on the creamy white of the menu how little those words conveyed to the bulk of the imperfectly educated diners. And yet how much specialised effort had been lavished, how much carefully treasured lore had been ungarnered, before those six words could be written. In the Department of Deux-Sèvres ducklings had lived peculiar and beautiful lives and died in the odour of satiety to furnish the main theme of the dish; champignons, which even a purist for Saxon English would have hesitated to address as mushrooms, had contributed their languorous atrophied bodies to the garnishing, and a sauce devised in the twilight reign of the Fifteenth Louis had been summoned back from the imperishable past to take its part in the wonderful confection. Thus far had human effort laboured to achieve the desired result; the rest had been left to human genius – the genius of Aristide Saucourt.

'And now the moment had arrived for the serving of the great dish, the dish which world-weary Grand Dukes and market-obsessed money magnates counted among their happiest memories. And at the same moment something else happened. The leader of the highly

52

salaried orchestra placed his violin caressingly against his chin, lowered his eyelids, and floated into a sea of melody.

'"Hark!"' said most of the diners, 'he is playing "The Chaplet".'

'They knew it was "The Chaplet" because they had heard it played at luncheon and afternoon tea, and at supper the night before, and had not had time to forget.

'"Yes, he is playing "The Chaplet",' they reassured one another. The general voice was unanimous on the subject. The orchestra had already played it eleven times that day, four times by desire and seven times from force of habit, but the familiar strains were greeted with the rapture due to a revelation. A murmur of much humming rose from half the tables in the room, and some of the more overwrought listeners laid down knife and fork in order to be able to burst in with loud clappings at the earliest permissible moment.

'And the Canetons à la mode d'Amblève? In stupefied, sickened wonder Aristide watched them grow cold in total neglect, or suffer the almost worse indignity of perfunctory pecking and listless munching while the banqueters lavished their approval and applause on the music-makers. Calves' liver and bacon, with parsley sauce, could hardly have figured more ignominiously in the evening's entertainment. And while the master of culinary art leaned back against the sheltering pillar, choking with a horrible brain-searing rage that could find no outlet for its agony, the orchestra leader was bowing his acknowledgments of the hand-clappings that rose in a storm around him. Turning to his colleagues he nodded the signal for an encore. But before the violin had been lifted anew into position there came from the shadow of the pillar an explosive negative.

'"Noh! Noh! You do not play thot again!"

'The musician turned in furious astonishment. Had he taken warning from the look in the other man's eyes he might have acted differently. But the admiring plaudits were ringing in his ears, and he snarled out sharply, "That is for me to decide."

'"Noh! You play thot never again," shouted the *chef*, and the next moment he had flung himself violently upon the loathed being who had supplanted him in the world's esteem. A large metal tureen, filled to the brim with steaming soup, had just been placed on a side table in readiness for a late party of diners; before the waiting staff or the guests had time to realise what was happening, Aristide had dragged his struggling victim up to the table and plunged his head deep down into the almost boiling contents of the tureen. At the further end of the room the diners were still spasmodically applauding in view of an encore.

'Whether the leader of the orchestra died from drowning by soup, or from the shock to his professional vanity, or was scalded to death, the doctors were never wholly able to agree. Monsieur Aristide Saucourt, who now lives in complete retirement, always inclined to the drowning theory.'

Saki: *The Chaplet*

ROMAN BANQUETS

Odours from the altars of the gods

At the farther end of this bland apartment, fragrant with the rare woods of the old inlaid panelling, the falling of aromatic oil from the ready-lighted lamps, the iris-root clinging to the dresses of the guests, as with odours from the altars of the gods, the supper-table was spread, in all the daintiness characteristic of the agreeable *petit-maître*, who entertained. He was already most carefully dressed, but, like Martial's Stella, perhaps consciously, meant to change his attire once and again during the banquet; in the last instance, for an ancient vesture (object of much rivalry among the young men of fashion, at that great sale of the imperial wardrobes), a toga, of altogether lost hue and texture. He wore it with a grace which became the leader of a thrilling movement then on foot for the restoration of that disused garment, in which, laying aside the customary evening dress, all the visitors were requested to appear, setting off the delicate sinuosities and well-disposed 'golden ways' of its folds, with harmoniously tinted flowers. The opulent sunset, blending pleasantly with artificial light, fell across the quiet ancestral effigies of old consular dignitaries, along the wide floor strewn with sawdust of sandal-wood, and lost itself in the heap of cool coronals, lying ready for the foreheads of the guests on a sideboard of old citron. The crystal vessels darkened with old wine, the hues of the early autumn fruit – mulberries, pomegranates, and grapes that had long been hanging under careful protection upon the vines, were almost as much a feast for the eye as the dusky fires of the rare twelve-petalled roses. A favourite animal, white as snow, brought by one of the visitors, purred its way gracefully among the wine-cups, coaxed onward from place to place by those at table, as they reclined easily on their cushions of German eider-down, spread over the long-legged, carved couches.

A highly refined modification of the *acroama* – a musical performance during supper for the diversion of the guests – was presently heard hovering round the place, soothingly, and so unobtrusively that the company could not guess, and did not like to ask, whether or not it had been designed by their entertainer. They inclined on the whole to think it some wonderful peasant-music peculiar to that wild neighbourhood, turning, as it did now and then, to a solitary reed-note, like a bird's, while it wandered into the distance. It wandered quite away at last, as darkness with a bolder lamplight came on, and made way for another sort of entertainment. An odd, rapid, phantasmal glitter, advancing from the garden by torchlight, defined itself, as it came nearer, into a dance of young men in armour. Arrived at length in a portico, open to the supper chamber, they contrived that their mechanical march-movement should fall out into a kind of highly expressive dramatic action; and with the utmost possible emphasis of dumb motion, their long swords weaving a silvery network in the air, they danced the *Death of Paris*.

Walter Pater: *Marius the Epicurean*

A succession of suppers

Philotas, a physician of Amphissa, who was at that time pursuing his studies in Alexandria, told my grandfather Lamprias that, being acquainted with one of Antony's cooks, he was invited to see the preparations for supper. When he came into the kitchen, besides an infinite variety of other provisions, he observed eight wild boars roasting whole; and expressed his surprise at the number of the company for whom this enormous provision must have been made. The cook laughed, and said that the company did not exceed twelve; but that, as every dish was to be roasted to a single turn, and as Antony was uncertain as to the time when he would sup, particularly if an extraordinary bottle was going round, it was necessary to have a succession of suppers.

Plutarch: *Parallel Lives*

Trimalchio's feast

Finally we took our places. Boys from Alexandria poured iced water over our hands. Others followed them and attended to our feet, removing any hangnails with great skill. But they were not quiet even during this troublesome operation: they sang away at their work. I wanted to find out if the whole staff were singers, so I asked for a drink. In a flash a boy was there, singing in a shrill voice while he attended to me – and anyone else who was asked to bring something did the same. It was more like a musical comedy than a respectable dinner party.

Some extremely elegant hors d'oeuvre were served at this point – by now everyone had taken his place with the exception of Trimalchio, for whom, strangely enough, the place at the top was reserved. The dishes for the first course included an ass of Corinthian bronze with two panniers, white olives on one side and black on the other. Over the ass were two pieces of plate, with Trimalchio's name and the weight of the silver inscribed on the rims. There were some small iron frames shaped like bridges supporting dormice sprinkled with honey and poppy seed. There were steaming hot sausages too, on a silver gridiron with damsons and pomegranate seeds underneath.

We were in the middle of these elegant dishes when Trimalchio himself was carried in to the sound of music and set down on a pile of tightly stuffed cushions. The sight of him drew an astonished laugh from the guests. His cropped head stuck out from a scarlet coat; his neck was well muffled up and he had put round it a napkin with a broad purple stripe and tassels dangling here and there. On the little finger of his left hand he wore a heavy gilt ring and a smaller one on the last joint of the next finger. This I thought was solid gold, but actually it was studded with little iron stars. And to show off even more of his jewellery, he had his right arm bare and set off by a gold armlet and an ivory circlet fastened with a gleaming metal plate.

After picking his teeth with a silver toothpick, he began: 'My friends, I wasn't keen to come into the dining room yet. But if I stayed away any more, I would have kept you back so I've deprived myself of all my little pleasures for you. However, you'll allow me to finish my game.'

A boy was at his heels with a board of terebinth wood with glass squares, and I noticed the very last word in luxury – instead of white and black pieces he had gold and silver coins. While he was swearing away like a trooper over his game and we were still on the hors d'oeuvre, a tray was brought in with a basket on it. There sat a wooden hen, its wings spread round it the way hens are when they are broody. Two slaves hurried up and as the orchestra played a tune they began searching through the straw and dug out peahens' eggs, which they distributed to the guests.

Trimalchio turned to look at this little scene and said: 'My friends, I gave orders for that bird to sit on some peahens' eggs. I hope to goodness they are not starting to hatch. However, let's try them and see if they are still soft.'

We took up our spoons (weighing at least half a pound each) and cracked the eggs, which were made of rich pastry. To tell the truth, I nearly threw away my share, as the chicken seemed already formed. But I heard a guest who was an old hand say: 'There should be something good here.' So I searched the shell with my fingers and found the plumpest little figpecker, all covered with yolk and seasoned with pepper.

Petronius: *The Satyricon* (translated by J. P. Sullivan)

À LA CARTE

A light snack in Davy Byrne's

He came out into clearer air and turned back towards Grafton street. Eat or be eaten. Kill! Kill!

Suppose that communal kitchen years to come perhaps. All trotting down with porringers and tommy-cans to be filled. Devour contents in the street. John Howard Parnell example the provost of Trinity every mother's son don't talk of your provosts and provost of Trinity women and children, cabmen, priests, parsons, fieldmarshals, archbishops. From Ailesbury road, Clyde road, artisans' dwellings, north Dublin union, lord mayor in his gingerbread coach, old queen in a bath-chair. My plate's empty. After you with our incorporated drinkingcup. Like sir Philip Crampton's fountain. Rub off the microbes with your handkerchief. Next chap rubs on a new batch with his. Father O'Flynn would make hares of them all. Have rows all the same. All for number one. Children fighting for the scrapings of the pot. Want a soup pot as big as the Phoenix Park. Harpooning flitches and hindquarters out of it. Hate people all round you. City Arms hotel *table d'hôte* she called it. Soup, joint and sweet. Never know whose thoughts you're chewing. Then who'd wash up all the plates and forks? Might be all feeding on tabloids that time. Teeth getting worse and worse.

After all there's a lot in that vegetarian fine flavour of things from the earth garlic, of course, it stinks Italian organgrinders crisp of onions, mushrooms truffles. Pain to animal too. Pluck and draw fowl. Wretched brutes there at the cattlemarket waiting for the poleaxe to split their skulls open. Moo. Poor trembling calves. Meh. Staggering bob. Bubble and squeak. Butchers' buckets wobble lights. Give us that brisket off the hook. Plup. Rawhead and bloody bones. Flayed glasseyed sheep hung from their haunches, sheepsnouts bloody-papered snivelling nosejam on sawdust. Top and lashers going out. Don't maul them pieces, young one.

Hot fresh blood they prescribe for decline. Blood always needed.

Insidious. Lick it up, smoking hot, thick sugary. Famished ghosts.

Ah, I'm hungry.

He entered Davy Byrne's. Moral pub. He doesn't chat. Stands a drink now and then. But in leapyear once in four. Cashed a cheque for me once.

What will I take now? He drew his watch. Let me see now. Shandygaff?

– Hellow, Bloom! Nosey Flynn said from his nook.

– Hello, Flynn.

– How's things?

– Tiptop . . . Let me see. I'll take a glass of burgundy and . . . let me see.

Sardines on the shelves. Almost taste them by looking. Sandwich? Ham and his descendants mustered and bred there. Potted meats. What is home without Plumtree's potted meat? Incomplete. What a stupid ad! Under the obituary notices they stuck it. All up a plumtree. Dignam's potted meat. Cannibals would with lemon and rice. White missionary too salty. Like pickled pork. Expect the chief consumes the parts of honour. Ought to be tough from exercise. His wives in a row to watch the effect. *There was a right royal old nigger. Who ate or something the somethings of the reverend Mr MacTrigger.* With it an abode of bliss. Lord knows what concoction. Cauls mouldy tripes windpipes faked and minced up. Puzzle find the meat. Kosher. No meat and milk together. Hygiene that was what they call now. Yom Kippur fast spring cleaning of inside. Peace and war depend on some fellow's digestion. Religions. Christmas turkeys and geese. Slaughter of innocents. Eat, drink and be merry. Then casual wards full after. Heads bandaged. Cheese digests all but itself. Mighty cheese.

– Have you a cheese sandwich?

– Yes, sir.

Like a few olives too if they had them. Italian I prefer. Good glass of burgundy; take away that. Lubricate. A nice salad, cool as a cucumber. Tom Kernan can dress. Puts gusto into it. Pure olive oil. Milly served me that cutlet with a sprig of parsley. Take one Spanish onion. God made food, the devil the cooks. Devilled crab.

– Wife well?

– Quite well, thanks . . . A cheese sandwich, then. Gorgonzola, have you?

– Yes, sir.

À La Carte

Nosey Flynn sipped his grog.

– Doing any singing those times?

Look at his mouth. Could whistle in his own ear. Flap ears to match. Music. Knows as much about it as my coachman. Still better tell him. Does no harm. Free ad.

– She's engaged for a big tour end of this month. You may have heard perhaps.

– No. O, that's the style. Who's getting it up?

The curate served.

– How much is that?

– Seven d., sir . . . Thank you, sir.

Mr Bloom cut his sandwich into slender strips. *Mr MacTrigger.* Easier than the dreamy creamy stuff. *His five hundred wives. Had the time of their lives.*

– Mustard, sir?

– Thank you.

He studded under each lifted strip yellow blobs. *Their lives.* I have it. *It grew bigger and bigger and bigger.*

– Getting it up? he said. Well, it's like a company idea, you see. Part shares and part profits.

– Ay, now I remember, Nosey Flynn said, putting his hand in his pocket to scratch his groin. Who is this was telling me? Isn't Blazes Boylan mixed up in it?

A warm shock of air heat of mustard hauched on Mr Bloom's heart. He raised his eyes and met the stare of a bilious clock. Two. Pub clock five minutes fast. Time going on. Hands moving. Two. Not yet.

James Joyce: *Ulysses*

A scratch embellishes an empty face

It was a bright day; the slanting rays of the winter sun peered through the icy windows. On the table, laid for supper, dimly shone pewter cups, a decanter of golden kvass, and another of Grandfather's dark green vodka, distilled from cowslip and St John's wort. Through the thawed patches on the window I could see the dazzling white snow on the roofs, forming sparkling silver caps on the fences and starling-box. My birds played in sunlight-flooded cages which hung from the window joists. The gay, tame chaffinches twittered merrily, the bullfinches chirped, and the goldfinch was overflowing with song. But that silvery day, so bright and full of music, did not raise my spirits. I did not want that day or anything else. I suddenly decided to set all the birds free and was just taking the cages down when in ran Grandmother, slapping her sides and swearing as she rushed to the stove:

'Damn and blast all of you! You old fool, Akulina! . . .'

She rescued a pie from the oven, poked the crust with her finger and spat in anger.

'It's burnt. To hell with the whole damned lot of you. And what are you goggling about, you owl? I'd like to smash you all up, like cracked cups.'

And she burst out crying, turning the pie from side to side, sticking her fingers in its dry crusts; large tears slopped down on them.

Grandfather came with Mother into the kitchen. She flung the pie on the table, making the plates jump.

'All because of you! May you go penniless!'

My mother, gay and unperturbed, embraced her and tried to calm her down. My dishevelled and tired-looking grandfather sat at the table, tucked a serviette round his neck, blinked his swollen eyes in the sunlight, and muttered:

'What's all the fuss? We've had pies before. God's a miser – gives you minutes in return for years, and without any interest. Sit down, Varya, that's right.'

He seemed to have lost his reason, and throughout supper talked about God, about the impious Ahab, about a father's hard lot.

'Get on with your supper and stop talking so much!'

Mother was in a joking mood and her clear eyes sparkled.

'Were you frightened just now?' she said as she nudged me.

No, I wasn't frightened, but now I felt ill, on edge, and mystified by everything that had happened.

The meal, as usual on Sundays, was interminable and heavy, and my grandparents and mother didn't seem the same people who half an hour before had been shouting at each other, were at each other's throats and were all tears and sobbing. And I couldn't believe any longer that all this was in earnest and that tears came hard to them. All those tears and shouts, and all the suffering they inflicted on each other, all those conflicts that died away just as quickly as they flared up, had now become an accepted part of my life, disturbed me less and less, and hardly left any impression. Long afterwards I understood that to Russians, through the poverty and squalor of their lives, suffering comes as a diversion, is turned into a game and they play at it like children and rarely feel ashamed of their misfortune. In the monotony of everyday existence grief comes as a holiday, and a fire is an entertainment. A scratch embellishes an empty face.

Maxim Gorky: *My Childhood*

A wholesome supper

She was so busy in admiring those soft blue eyes, in talking and listening, and forming all these schemes in the in-betweens, that the evening flew away at a very unusual rate; and the supper-table, which always closed such parties, and for which she had been used to sit and watch the due time, was all set out and ready, and moved forwards to the fire, before she was aware. With an alacrity beyond the common impulse of a spirit which yet was never indifferent to the credit of doing every thing well and attentively, with the real good-will of a mind delighted with its own ideas, did she then do all the honours of the meal, and help and recommend the minced chicken and scalloped oysters with an urgency which she knew would be acceptable to the early hours and civil scruples of their guests.

Upon such occasions poor Mr Woodhouse's feelings were in sad warfare. He loved to have the cloth laid, because it had been the fashion of his youth; but his conviction of suppers being very unwholesome made him rather sorry to see any thing put on it; and while his hospitality would have welcomed his visitors to every thing, his care for their health made him grieve that they would eat.

Such another small basin of thin gruel as his own, was all that he could, with thorough self-approbation, recommend, though he might constrain himself, while the ladies were comfortably clearing the nicer things, to say:

'Mrs Bates, let me propose your venturing on one of these eggs. An egg boiled very soft is not unwholesome. Serle understands boiling an egg better than any body. I would not recommend an egg boiled by any body else – but you need not be afraid – they are very small, you see – one of our small eggs will not hurt you. Miss Bates, let Emma help you to a *little* bit of tart – a *very* little bit. Ours are all apple tarts. You need not be afraid of unwholesome preserves here. I do not advise the custard. Mrs Goddard, what say you to *half* a glass of wine? A *small* half glass – put into a tumbler of water? I do not think it could disagree with you.'

Emma allowed her father to talk – but supplied her visitors in a much more satisfactory style; and on the present evening had particular pleasure in sending them away happy. The happiness of Miss Smith was quite equal to her intentions. Miss Woodhouse was so great a personage in Highbury, that the prospect of the introduction had given as much panic as pleasure – but the humble, grateful, little girl went off with highly gratified feelings, delighted with the affability with which Miss Woodhouse had treated her all the evening, and actually shaken hands with her at last!

Jane Austen: *Emma*

No man eat more heartily

When we entered Mr Dilly's drawing-room, he found himself in the midst of a company he did not know. I kept myself snug and silent, watching how he would conduct himself. I observed him whispering to Mr Dilly, 'Who is that gentleman, Sir?' – 'Mr Arthur Lee.' JOHNSON. 'Too, too, too' (under his breath), which was one of his habitual mutterings. Mr Arthur Lee could not but be very obnoxious to Johnson, for he was not only a *patriot*, but an *American*. 'And who is the gentleman in lace?' – 'Mr Wilkes, Sir.' This information confounded him still more; he had some difficulty to restrain himself, and, taking up a book, sat down upon a window-seat and read, or at least kept his eye upon it intently for some time, till he composed himself. His feelings, I dare say, were awkward enough. But he no doubt recollected having rated me for supposing that he could be at all disconcerted by any company, and he therefore resolutely set himself to behave quite as an easy man of the world, who could adapt himself at once to the disposition and manners of those whom he might chance to meet.

The cheering sound of 'Dinner is upon the table,' dissolved his reverie, and we *all* sat down without any symptom of ill humour. There were present, beside Mr Wilkes and Mr Arthur Lee, who was an old companion of mine when he studied physic at Edinburgh, Mr (now Sir John) Miller, Dr Lettsom, and Mr Slater, the druggist. Mr Wilkes placed himself next to Dr Johnson, and behaved to him with so much attention and politeness, that he gained upon him insensibly. No man eat more heartily than Johnson, or loved better what was nice and delicate. Mr Wilkes was very assiduous in helping him to some fine veal. 'Pray give me leave, Sir – It is better here – A little of the brown – Some fat, Sir – A little of the stuffing – Some gravy – Let me have the pleasure of giving you some butter – Allow me to recommend a squeeze of this orange; or the lemon, perhaps, may have more zest.' – 'Sir; sir, I am obliged to you, Sir,' cried Johnson, bowing, and turning his head to him with a look for some time of 'surly virtue', but, in a short while, of complacency.

James Boswell: *The Life of Samuel Johnson*

Gran turismo

His two battered suitcases came and he unpacked leisurely and then ordered from Room Service a bottle of the Taittinger Blanc de Blanc that he had made his traditional drink at Royale. When the bottle, in its frosted silver bucket, came, he drank a quarter of it rather fast and then went into the bathroom and had an ice-cold shower and washed his hair with Pinaud Elixir, that prince among shampoos, to get the dust of the roads out of it. Then he slipped on his dark-blue tropical worsted trousers, white sea-island cotton shirt, socks and black casual shoes (he abhorred shoe-laces), and went and sat at the window and looked out across the promenade to the sea and wondered where he would have dinner and what he would choose to eat.

James Bond was not a gourmet. In England he lived on grilled soles, œufs cocotte and cold roast beef with potato salad. But when travelling abroad, generally by himself, meals were a welcome break in the day, something to look forward to, something to break the tension of fast driving, with its risks taken or avoided, the narrow squeaks, the permanent background of concern for the fitness of his machine. In fact, at this moment, after covering the long stretch from the Italian frontier at Ventimiglia in a comfortable three days (God knew there was no reason to hurry back to Headquarters!), he was fed to the teeth with the sucker-traps for gourmandising tourists. The 'Hostelleries', the 'Vieilles Auberges', the 'Relais Fleuris' – he had had the lot. He had had their 'Bonnes Tables', and their 'Fines Bouteilles'. He had had their 'Spécialités du Chef' – generally a rich sauce of cream and wine and a few button mushrooms concealing poor quality meat or fish. He had had the whole lip-smacking ritual of winemanship and foodmanship and, incidentally, he had had quite enough of the Bisodol that went with it!

The French belly-religion had delivered its final kick at him the night before. Wishing to avoid Orléans, he had stopped south of this uninspiring city and had chosen a mock-Breton Auberge on the south bank of the Loire, despite its profusion of window-boxes and sham beams, ignoring the china cat pursuing the china bird across its gabled roof, because it was right on the edge of the Loire – perhaps Bond's favourite river in the world. He had stoically accepted the hammered copper warming pans, brass cooking utensils and other antique bogosities that cluttered the walls of the entrance hall, had left his bag in his room and had gone for an agreeable walk along the softly running, swallow-skimmed river. The dining-room, in which he was one of a small handful of tourists, had sounded the alarm. Above a fire-place of electric logs and over-polished fire-irons there had hung a coloured plaster escutcheon bearing the dread device: ICY DOULCE FRANCE. All the plates, of some hideous local ware, bore the jingle, irritatingly inscrutable, 'Jamais en Vain, Toujours en Vin', and the surly waiter, stale with 'fin de saison', had served him with the fly-walk of the Pâté Maison (sent back for a new slice) and a Poularde à la crème that was the only genuine antique in the place. Bond had moodily washed down this sleazy provender with a bottle of instant Pouilly Fuissé and was finally insulted the next morning by a bill for the meal in excess of five pounds.

It was to efface all these dyspeptic memories that Bond now sat at his window, sipped his Taittinger and weighed up the pros and cons of the local eating places and wondered what dishes it would be best to gamble on. He finally chose one of his favourite restaurants in France, a modest establishment, unpromisingly placed exactly opposite the railway station of Étaples, rang up his old friend Monsieur Bécaud for a table and, two hours later, was motoring back to the Casino with Turbot poché, sauce mousseline, and half the best roast partridge he had eaten in his life, under his belt.

Greatly encouraged, and further stimulated by half a bottle of Mouton Rothschild '53 and a glass of ten-year-old Calvados with his three cups of coffee, he went cheerfully up the thronged steps of the Casino with the absolute certitude that this was going to be a night to remember.

Ian Fleming: *On Her Majesty's Secret Service*

Terrines and galantines

There was, however, a market. The square, the usual small-town
assembly of cafés and banks in higgledy-piggledy buildings topped
by squinting dormers narrowing upwards to a clocktower with a
hoarse bell that announced the quarters as if they had happened long
ago, was packed with stalls that heaped up on their boards the various
fecundities of this countryside, tomatoes, cheeses, hams, artichokes,
cherries, every monger pricing his goods lower than those of his
neighbour as noon approached, wives hustling and bridling for
preferential treatment under the stripes of shadow from makeshift
awnings, and at once Kestner began taking a professional interest.
He was hypnotised by the massed foods, and how it touched Tina
to see it! A fat terrine concentrated his eye as he mentally ticked off
the ingredients down to the last subtle pinch of spice. His face grew
solemn over a plump rounded pink ham bordered in black, from
which slivers of meat were curling deliciously off the slicer. He gazed
into the jellied depths of a brawn, nodding sagely, an old man who
had devoted his working life to the manufacture of such delicacies,
wondering if here in the south he had been outclassed, full of
admiration but also racked by doubt. Taking his arm, without
thinking, Tina squeezed it to her breast. 'Oh, do let's have a picnic,'
she said. 'I don't want to sit in a restaurant with you, other people
pricking up their ears at our language, and all that. Let's buy and buy
and buy. We can have a feast together. By a river. Let's find a river
bank, with some shade. We're on holiday.'

Kestner paused, stared at a galantine studded with olives which he
wished he had made, and nodded agreement, with both appetite and
gloom.

They shopped. They bought, wrapped in oiled paper, paper-
bagged, tucked into Tina's shoulder-bag, slipped into the baggy
pockets of Kestner's suit, far more food than they could possibly
consume. Kestner thought of Jannie's offerings, the brief hungry
respite from their acts of love, by streams, up gullies, in bed. Tina
imagined the open air, the long pause of noontide under the sun,
when people without conscience ate their fill and dozed in peace. The

cracked bell sounded another long-forgotten quarter. The square cleared of wives as the flies gathered and the banks shut and the cafés filled; the sun struck daggers of light through glasses of white wine. And at the last moment, before everyone vanished into shuttered gloom to fall upon excessive meals and leave the afternoon to look after itself, they plunged, parcelled to the eyebrows, into a cavern of a shop and bought, at Tina's request, a choice of local vintages. They would have to eat with their fingers and drink from the bottle.

David Hughes: *The Pork Butcher*

Saddle of lamb

Family dinners of the Forsytes observe certain traditions. There are, for instance, no *hors d'œuvres*. The reason for this is unknown. Theory among the younger members traces it to the disgraceful price of oysters; it is more probably due to a desire to come to the point, to a good practical sense deciding at once that *hors d'œuvres* are but poor things. The Jameses alone, unable to withstand a custom almost universal in Park Lane, are now and then unfaithful.

A silent, almost morose, inattention to each other succeeds to the subsidence into their seats, lasting till well into the first entrée, but interspersed with remarks such as, 'Tom's bad again; I can't tell what's the matter with him!' – 'I suppose Ann doesn't come down in the mornings?' – 'What's the name of your doctor, Fanny? Stubbs? He's a quack!' – 'Winifred? She's got too many children. Four, isn't it? She's as thin as a lath!' – 'What d'you give for this sherry, Swithin? Too dry for me!'

With the second glass of champagne, a kind of hum makes itself heard, which, when divested of casual accessories and resolved into its primal element, is found to be James telling a story, and this goes on for a long time, encroaching sometimes even upon what must universally be recognised as the crowning point of a Forsyte feast – 'the saddle of mutton'.

À *La Carte*

No Forsyte has given a dinner without providing a saddle of mutton. There is something in its succulent solidity which makes it suitable to people 'of a certain position'. It is nourishing and – tasty; the sort of thing a man remembers eating. It has a past and a future, like a deposit paid into a bank; and it is something that can be argued about.

Each branch of the family tenaciously held to a particular locality – old Jolyon swearing by Dartmoor, James by Welsh, Swithin by Southdown, Nicholas maintaining that people might sneer, but there was nothing like New Zealand. As for Roger, the 'original' of the brothers, he had been obliged to invent a locality of his own, and with an ingenuity worthy of a man who had devised a new profession for his sons, he had discovered a shop where they sold German; on being remonstrated with, he had proved his point by producing a butcher's bill, which showed that he paid more than any of the others. It was on this occasion that old Jolyon, turning to June, had said in one of his bursts of philosophy:

'You may depend upon it, they're a cranky lot, the Forsytes – and you'll find it out, as you grow older!'

Timothy alone held apart, for though he ate saddle of mutton heartily, he was, he said, afraid of it.

To anyone interested psychologically in Forsytes, this great saddle-of-mutton trait is of prime importance; not only does it illustrate their tenacity, both collectively and as individuals, but it marks them as belonging in fibre and instincts to that great class which believes in nourishment and flavour, and yields to no sentimental craving for beauty.

John Galsworthy: *The Man of Property*

Eddie's cake

Eddie watched his stove like a mother hen. He was baking a cake in a wash-basin. The recipe was guaranteed not to fail by the company which made the shortening. But from the first the cake had acted strangely. When the batter was completed it writhed and panted as though animals were squirming and crawling inside it. Once in the oven it put up a bubble like a baseball which grew tight and shiny and then collapsed with a hissing sound. This left such a crater that Eddie made a new batch of batter and filled in the hole. And now the cake was behaving very curiously, for while the bottom was burning and sending out a black smoke the top was rising and falling glueyly with a series of little explosions.

When Eddie finally put it out to cool, it looked like one of Bel Geddes's miniatures of a battlefield on a lava bed.

This cake was not fortunate, for while the boys were decorating the laboratory Darling ate what she could of it, was sick on it, and finally curled up in its still warm dough and went to sleep.

John Steinbeck: *Cannery Row*

The Custom House Inspector

One point, in which he had vastly the advantage over his four-footed brethren, was his ability to recollect the good dinners which it had made no small portion of the happiness of his life to eat. His gourmandism was a highly agreeable trait; and to hear him talk of roast meat was as appetising as a pickle or an oyster. As he possessed no higher attribute, and neither sacrificed nor vitiated any spiritual endowment by devoting all his energies and ingenuities to subserve the delight and profit of his maw, it always pleased and satisfied me to hear him expatiate on fish, poultry, and butcher's meat, and the most eligible methods of preparing them for the table. His reminiscences of good cheer, however ancient the date of the actual banquet, seemed to bring the savor of pig or turkey under one's very nostrils. There were flavors on his palate, that had lingered there not less than sixty or seventy years, and were still apparently as fresh as that of the mutton chop which he had just devoured for his breakfast. I have heard him smack his lips over dinners, every guest at which, except himself, had long been food for worms. It was marvellous to observe how the ghosts of bygone meals were continually rising up before him; not in anger or retribution, but as if grateful for his former appreciation, and seeking to repudiate an endless series of enjoyment, at once shadowy and sensual. A tenderloin of beef, a hind-quarter of veal, a sparerib of pork, a particular chicken, or a remarkably praiseworthy turkey, which had perhaps adorned his board in the days of the elder Adams, would be remembered; while all the subsequent experience of our race, and all the events that brightened or darkened his individual career, had gone over him with as little permanent effect as the passing breeze. The chief tragic event of the old man's life, so far as I could judge, was his mishap with a certain goose, which lived and died some twenty or forty years ago; a goose of most promising figure, but which, at table, proved so inveterately tough that the carving knife would make no impression on its carcass, and it could only be divided with an axe and handsaw.

Nathaniel Hawthorne: *The Scarlet Letter*

STILL LIFE

The rites of the palate

I would now happily remain at the table while it was being cleared, and, if it was not a moment at which the girls of the little band might be passing, it was no longer solely towards the sea that I would turn my eyes. Since I had seen such things depicted in water-colours by Elstir, I sought to find again in reality, I cherished as though for their poetic beauty, the broken gestures of the knives still lying across one another, the swollen convexity of a discarded napkin into which the sun introduced a patch of yellow velvet, the half-empty glass which thus showed to greater advantage the noble sweep of its curved sides and, in the heart of its translucent crystal, clear as frozen daylight, some dregs of wine, dark but glittering with reflected lights, the displacement of solid objects, the transmutation of liquids by the effect of light and shade, the shifting colours of the plums which passed from green to blue and from blue to golden yellow in the half-plundered dish, the chairs, like a group of old ladies, that came twice daily to take their places round the white cloth spread on the table as on an altar at which were celebrated the rites of the palate, and where in the hollows of the oyster-shells a few drops of lustral water had remained as in tiny holy water stoups of stone; I tried to find beauty there where I had never imagined before that it could exist, in the most ordinary things, in the profundities of 'still life'.

Marcel Proust: *Remembrance of Things Past*
(translated by C. K. Scott-Moncrieff and Terence Kilmartin)

A party round a table

Now eight candles were stood down the table, and after the first stoop the flames stood upright and drew with them into visibility the long table entire, and in the middle a yellow and purple dish of fruit. What had she done with it, Mrs Ramsay wondered, for Rose's arrangement of the grapes and pears, of the horny pink-lined shell, of the bananas, made her think of a trophy fetched from the bottom of the sea, of Neptune's banquet, of the bunch that hangs with vine leaves over the shoulder of Bacchus (in some picture), among the leopard skins and the torches lolloping red and gold . . . Thus brought up suddenly into the light it seemed possessed of great size and depth, was like a world in which one could take one's staff and climb up hills, she thought, and go down into valleys, and to her pleasure (for it brought them into sympathy momentarily) she saw that Augustus too feasted his eyes on the same plate of fruit, plunged in, broke off a bloom there, a tassel here, and returned, after feasting, to his hive. That was his way of looking, different from hers. But looking together united them.

Now all the candles were lit, and the faces on both sides of the table were brought nearer by the candle light, and composed, as they had not been in the twilight, into a party round a table, for the night was now shut off by panes of glass, which, far from giving any accurate view of the outside world, rippled it so strangely that here, inside the room, seemed to be order and dry land; there, outside, a reflection in which things wavered and vanished, waterily.

Virginia Woolf: *To the Lighthouse*

Delicates in baskets bright

XXX

And still she slept an azure-lidded sleep,
In blanched linen, smooth, and lavender'd,
While he from forth the closet brought a heap
Of candied apple, quince, and plum, and gourd;
With jellies soother than the creamy curd,
And lucent syrops, tinct with cinnamon;
Manna and dates, in argosy transferr'd
.From Fez; and spiced dainties, every one,
From silken Samarcand to cedar'd Lebanon.

XXXI

These delicates he heap'd with glowing hand
On golden dishes and in baskets bright
Of wreathed silver: sumptuous they stand
In the retired quiet of the night,
Filling the chilly room with perfume light. –

John Keats: *The Eve of St Agnes*

COUNTRY COOKING

Dinner at Grasmere

After as good and well-dressed a dinner, at Robert Newton's, as a man could wish, we set out to surmount the steep ascent of Helm Crag; but the dinner was so cheap, I must mention what it consisted of:

Roast pike, stuffed,
A boiled fowl,
Veal-cutlets and ham,
Beans and bacon,
Cabbage,
Pease and potatoes,
Anchovy sauce,
Parsley and butter,
Plain butter,
Butter and cheese,
Wheat bread and oak cake,
Three cups of preserved gooseberries, with a bowl of rich cream in the centre:
For two people, at ten-pence a head.

Joseph Budworth: *A Fortnight's Ramble to the Lakes*, from *The Lake District*, edited by Norman Nicholson

Mr Badger's kitchen

The floor was well-worn red brick, and on the wide hearth burnt a fire of logs, between two attractive chimney-corners tucked away in the wall, well out of any suspicion of draught. A couple of high-backed settles, facing each other on either side of the fire, gave further sitting accommodation for the sociably disposed. In the middle of the room stood a long table of plain boards placed on trestles, with benches down each side. At one end of it, where an arm-chair stood pushed back, were spread the remains of the Badger's plain but ample supper. Rows of spotless plates winked from the shelves of the dresser at the far end of the room, and from the rafters overhead hung hams, bundles of dried herbs, nets of onions, and baskets of eggs. It seemed a place where heroes could fitly feast after victory, where weary harvesters could line up in scores along the table and keep their Harvest Home with mirth and song, or where two or three friends of simple tastes could sit about as they pleased and eat and smoke and talk in comfort and contentment. The ruddy brick floor smiled up at the smoky ceiling; the oaken settles, shiny with long wear, exchanged cheerful glances with each other; plates on the dresser grinned at pots on the shelf, and the merry firelight flickered and played over everything without distinction.

The kindly Badger thrust them down on a settle to toast themselves at the fire, and bade them remove their wet coats and boots. Then he fetched them dressing-gowns and slippers, and himself bathed the Mole's shin with warm water and mended the cut with sticking-plaster till the whole thing was just as good as new, if not better. In the embracing light and warmth, warm and dry at last, with weary legs propped up in front of them, and a suggestive clink of plates being arranged on the table behind, it seemed to the storm-driven animals, now in safe anchorage, that the cold and trackless Wild Wood just left outside was miles and miles away, and all that they had suffered in it a half-forgotten dream.

When at last they were thoroughly toasted, the Badger summoned them to the table, where he had been busy laying a repast. They had felt pretty hungry before, but when they actually saw at last the supper that was spread for them, really it seemed only a question of what they should attack first where all was so attractive, and whether the other things would obligingly wait for them till they had time to give them attention. Conversation was impossible for a long time; and when it was slowly resumed, it was that regrettable sort of conversation that results from talking with your mouth full.

Kenneth Grahame: *The Wind in the Willows*

The Flower Show match

The Luncheon Tent stood on that part of the field where the Flower Show ended and the swings and roundabouts began. Although the meal was an informal affair, there was a shy solemnity in the faces of most of the players as they filtered out of the bright sunshine into the sultry, half-lit interior, where the perspiring landlord of the 'Chequers' and his buxom wife were bustling about at the climax of their preparations. While the cricketers were shuffling themselves awkwardly into their places, the brawny barman (who seemed to take catering less seriously than his employers) sharpened the carving-knife on a steel prong with a rasping sound that set one's teeth on edge while predicting satisfactory slices of lamb and beef, to say nothing of veal and ham pie and a nice bit of gammon of bacon.

As soon as all were seated Dodd created silence by rapping the table; he then put on his churchwarden face and looked toward Parson Yalden, who was in readiness to take his cue. He enunciated the grace in slightly unparsonic tones, which implied that he was not only Rector of Rotherden, but also a full member of the MCC and first cousin once removed to Lord Chatwynd. Parson Yalden's parishioners occasionally complained that he paid more attention to cricket and pheasant shooting than was fit and proper. But as long as he could afford to keep a hard-working curate he rightly considered it his own affair if he chose to spend three days a week playing in club and country-house matches all over the county. His demeanour when keeping wicket for his own parish was both jaunty and magisterial, and he was renowned for the strident and obstreperous bellow to which he gave vent when he was trying to bluff a village umpire into giving a batsman out 'caught behind'. He was also known for his habit of genially engaging the batsman in conversation while the bowler was intent on getting him out, and I have heard of at least one occasion when he tried this little trick on the wrong man. The pestered batsman rounded on the rather foxy-faced clergyman with, 'I bin playing cricket nigh on thirty years, and parson or no parson, I take the liberty of telling you to hold your blasted gab.'

But I hurriedly dismissed this almost unthinkable anecdote when he turned his greenish eyes in my direction and hoped, in hearty and ingratiating tones, that I was 'going to show them a little crisp Ballboro' batting'.

The brisk clatter of knives and forks is now well started, and the barman is busy at his barrel. Conversation, however, is scanty, until Tom Seamark, who is always glad of a chance to favour the company with a sentiment, clears his throat impressively, elevates his tankard, fixes Jack Barchard with his gregarious regard, and remarks, 'I should like to say, sir, how very pleased and proud we all are to see you safe 'ome again in our midst.' Jack Barchard has recently returned from the Boer War where he served with the Yeomanry. The 'sentiment' is echoed from all parts of the table, and glasses are raised to him with a gruff 'Good 'ealth, sir,' or 'Right glad to see you back, Mr Barchard.' The returned warrior receives their congratulations with the utmost embarrassment. Taking a shy sip at my ginger-beer, I think how extraordinary it is to be sitting next to a man who has really been 'out in South Africa'. Barchard is a fair-haired young gentleman farmer. When the parson suggests that 'it must have been pretty tough work out there', he replies that he is thundering glad to be back among his fruit trees again, and this, apparently, is about all he has to say about the Boer War.

But when the meal was drawing to an end and I had finished my helping of cold cherry-tart, and the barman began to circulate with a wooden platter for collecting the half-crowns, I became agonisingly aware that I had come to the match without any money. I was getting into a panic while the plate came clinking along the table, but quiet Jack Barchard unconsciously saved the situation by putting down

five shillings and saying, 'All right, old chap, I'll stump up for both.'
Mumbling, 'Oh, that's jolly decent of you,' I wished I could have
followed him up a hill in a 'forlorn hope' . . . He told me, later on,
that he never set eyes on a Boer the whole time he was in South
Africa.

Siegfried Sassoon: *Memoirs of a Fox-hunting Man*

Bread, bacon and cider

'Come, shepherd, and drink. 'Tis gape and swaller with us – a drap
of sommit, but not of much account,' said the maltster, removing
from the fire his eyes, which were vermilion-red and bleared by
peering into it for so many years. 'Take up the God-forgive-me,
Jacob. See if 'tis warm, Jacob.'

Jacob stooped to the God-forgive-me, which was a two-handled
tall mug standing in the ashes, cracked and charred with heat: it was
rather furred with extraneous matter about the outside, especially in
the crevices of the handles, the innermost curves of which may not
have seen daylight for several years by reason of this encrustation
thereon – formed of ashes accidentally wetted with cider and baked
hard; but to the mind of any sensible drinker the cup was no worse
for that, being incontestably clean on the inside and about the rim.
It may be observed that such a class of mug is called a God-forgive-me
in Weatherbury and its vicinity for uncertain reasons; probably because its size makes any given toper feel ashamed of himself when he
sees its bottom in drinking it empty.

Jacob, on receiving the order to see if the liquor was warm enough,
placidly dipped his forefinger into it by way of thermometer, and
having pronounced it nearly of the proper degree, raised the cup and
very civilly attempted to dust some of the ashes from the bottom with
the skirt of his smock-frock, because Shepherd Oak was a stranger.

'A clane cup for the shepherd,' said the maltster commandingly.

'No – not at all,' said Gabriel, in a reproving tone of considerateness. 'I never fuss about dirt in its pure state, and when I know what sort it is.' Taking the mug he drank an inch or more from the depth of its contents, and duly passed it to the next man. 'I wouldn't think of giving such trouble to neighbours in washing up when there's so much work to be done in the world already,' continued Oak in a moister tone, after recovering from the stoppage of breath which is occasioned by pulls at large mugs.

'A right sensible man,' said Jacob.

'True, true; it can't be gainsaid!' observed a brisk young man – Mark Clark by name, a genial and pleasant gentleman, whom to meet anywhere in your travels was to know, to know was to drink with, and to drink with was, unfortunately, to pay for.

'And here's a mouthful of bread and bacon that mis'ess have sent, shepherd. The cider will go down better with a bit of victuals. Don't ye chaw quite close, shepherd, for I let the bacon fall in the road outside as I was bringing it along, and may be 'tis rather gritty. There, 'tis clane dirt; and we all know what that is, as you say, and you bain't a particular man we see, shepherd.'

'True, true – not at all,' said the friendly Oak.

'Don't let your teeth quite meet, and you won't feel the sandiness at all. Ah! 'tis wonderful what can be done by contrivance!'

'My own mind exactly, neighbour.'

'Ah, he's his grandfer's own grandson! – his grandfer were just such a nice unparticular man!' said the maltster.

Thomas Hardy: *Far from the Madding Crowd*

A table heaped with dainties

I remember once beneath the battlements of Oebalia,
Where dark Galaesus waters the golden fields of corn,
I saw an old man, a Corycian, who owned a few poor acres
Of land once derelict, useless for arable,

No good for grazing, unfit for the cultivation of vines.
But he laid out a kitchen garden in rows amid the brushwood,
Bordering it with white lilies, verbena, small-seeded poppy.
He was happy there as a king. He could go indoors at night
To a table heaped with dainties he never had to buy.
His the first rose of spring, the earliest apples in autumn:
And when grim winter still was splitting the rocks with cold
And holding the watercourses with curb of ice, already
That man would be cutting his soft-haired hyacinths,
   complaining
Of summer's backwardness and the west winds slow to come.
His bees were the first to breed.
Enriching him with huge swarms: he squeezed the frothy honey
Before anyone else from the combs: he had limes and a wealth
   of pine trees:
And all the early blossom, that clothed his trees with promise
Of an apple crop, by autumn had come to maturity.
He had a gift, too, for transplanting in rows the far-grown elm,
The hardwood pear, the blackthorn bearing its weight of sloes,
And the plane that already offered a pleasant shade for drinking.

Virgil: *The Georgics* (translated by C. Day Lewis)

Tom deserves his supper

'Cousin Tom,' said mother, and trying to get so that Annie and I
could not hear her; 'it would be a sad and unkinlike thing, for you
to despise our dwelling-house. We cannot entertain you, as the lordly
inns on the road do; and we have small change of victuals. But the
men will go home, being Saturday; and so you will have the fireside
all to yourself and the children. There are some few collops of red
deer's flesh, and a ham just down from the chimney, and some dried
salmon from Lynmouth weir, and cold roast-pig, and some oysters.
And if none of those be to your liking, we could roast two wood-

cocks in half an hour, and Annie would make the toast for them. And the good folk made some mistake last week, going up the country, and left a keg of old Holland cordial in the coving of the woodrick, having borrowed our Smiler, without asking leave. I fear there is something unrighteous about it. But what can a poor widow do? John Fry would have taken it, but for our Jack. Our Jack was a little too sharp for him.'

Ay, that I was; John Fry had got it, like a billet under his apron, going away in the grey of the morning, as if to kindle his fireplace. 'Why, John,' I said, 'what a heavy log! Let me have one end of it.' 'Thank'e, Jan, no need of thiccy,' he answered, turning his back to me; 'waife wanteth a log as will last all day, to kape the crock a zimmerin.' And he banged his gate upon my heels, to make me stop and rub them. 'Why, John,' said I, 'you'm got a log with round holes in the end of it. Who has been cutting gun-wads? Just lift your apron, or I will.'

But, to return to Tom Faggus – he stopped to sup that night with us, and took a little of every thing; a few oysters first, and then dried salmon, and then ham and eggs, done in small curled rashers, and then a few collops of venison toasted, and next to that a little cold roast-pig, and a wood-cock on toast to finish with, before the Schiedam and hot water. And having changed his wet things first, he seemed to be in fair appetite, and praised Annie's cooking mightily, with a relishing noise like a smack of his lips, and a rubbing of his hands together, whenever he could spare them.

R. D. Blackmore: *Lorna Doone*

CANNIBAL CORNER

The funeral feast of the Emperor Seth

The chiefs gave the sign for the feast to begin.

The company split up into groups, each round a cook-pot. Basil and Joab sat with the chiefs. They ate flat bread and meat, stewed to pulp among peppers and aromatic roots. Each dipped into the pot in rotation, plunging with his hands for the best scraps. A bowl of toddy circulated from lap to lap and great drops of sweat broke out on the brows of the mourners.

Dancing was resumed, faster this time and more clearly oblivious of fatigue. In emulation of the witch doctors, the tribesmen began slashing themselves on chest and arms with their hunting knives; blood and sweat mingled in shining rivulets over their dark skins. Now and then one of them would pitch forward on to his face and lie panting or roll stiff in a nervous seizure. Women joined in the dance, making another chain, circling in the reverse way to the men. They were dazed with drink, stamping themselves into ecstasy. The two chains jostled and combined. They shuffled together interlocked.

Basil drew back a little from the heat of the fire, his senses dazed by the crude spirit and the insistence of the music. In the shadows, in the extremities of the market-place, black figures sprawled and grunted, alone and in couples. Near him an elderly woman stamped and shuffled; suddenly she threw up her arms and fell to the ground in ecstasy. The hand-drums throbbed and pulsed; the flames leapt and showered the night with sparks.

The headman of Moshu sat where they had dined, nursing the bowl of toddy. He wore an Azanian white robe, splashed with gravy and spirit. His scalp was closely shaven; he nodded down to the lip of the bowl and drank. Then he clumsily offered it to Basil. Basil refused; he gaped and offered it again. Then took another draught himself. Then he nodded again and drew something from his bosom and put it on his head. 'Look,' he said. 'Pretty.'

It was a beret of pillar-box red. Through the stupor that was slowly mounting and encompassing his mind Basil recognised it. Prudence had worn it jauntily on the side of her head, running across the Legation lawn with the *Panorama of Life* under her arm. He shook the old fellow roughly by the shoulder.

'Where did you get that?'

'Pretty.'

'Where did you get it?'

'Pretty hat. It came in the great bird. The white woman wore it. On her head like this.' He giggled weakly and pulled it askew over his glistening pate.

'But the white woman. Where is she?'

But the headman was lapsing into coma. He said 'Pretty' again and turned up sightless eyes.

Basil shook him violently. 'Speak, you old fool. Where is the white woman?'

The headman grunted and stirred; then a flicker of consciousness revived in him. He raised his head. 'The white woman? Why, here,' he patted his distended paunch. 'You and I and the big chiefs – we have just eaten her.'

Then he fell forward into a sound sleep.

Evelyn Waugh: *Black Mischief*

Captain Murderer

The first diabolical character who intruded himself on my peaceful youth (as I called to mind that day at Dullborough) was a certain Captain Murderer. This wretch must have been an offshoot of the Blue Beard family, but I had no supicion of the consanguinity in those times. His warning name would seem to have awakened no general prejudice against him, for he was admitted into the best society, and possessed immense wealth. Captain Murderer's mission was matrimony, and the gratification of a cannibal appetite with tender brides. On his marriage morning, he always caused both sides of the way to church to be planted with curious flowers; and when his bride said, 'Dear Captain Murderer, I never saw flowers like these before: what are they called?' he answered, 'They are called Garnish for house-lamb,' and laughed at his ferocious practical joke in a horrid manner disquieting the minds of the noble bridal company, with a very sharp show of teeth, then displayed for the first time. He made love in a coach and six, and married in a coach and twelve, and all his horses were milk-white horses with one red spot on the back, which he caused to be hidden by the harness. For, the spot *would* come there, though every horse was milk-white when Captain Murderer bought him. And the spot was young bride's blood. (To this terrific point I am indebted for my first personal experience of a shudder and cold beads on the forehead.) When Captain Murderer had made an end of feasting and revelry, and had dismissed the noble guests, and was alone with his wife on the day month after their marriage, it was his whimsical custom to produce a golden rolling-pin and a silver pie-board. Now, there was this special feature in the Captain's court-ships, that he always asked if the young lady could make pie-crust; and, if she couldn't by nature or education, she was taught. Well! When the bride saw Captain Murderer produce the golden rolling-pin and silver pie-board, she remembered this, and turned up her laced-silk sleeves to make a pie. The Captain brought out a silver pie-dish of immense capacity, and the Captain brought out flour and butter and eggs and all things needful, except the inside of the pie; of materials for the staple of the pie itself, the Captain brought out none. Then said the lovely bride, 'Dear Captain Murderer, what pie is this to be?' He replied, 'A meat-pie.' Then said the lovely bride, 'Dear Captain Murderer, I see no meat.' The Captain humorously retorted, 'Look in the glass.' She looked in the glass, but still she saw no meat, and then the Captain roared with laughter, and, suddenly frowning and drawing his sword, bade her roll out the crust. So she rolled out the crust, dropping large tears upon it all the time because he was so cross, and when she had lined the dish with crust, and had cut the crust all ready to fit the top, the Captain called out, '*I* see the meat in the glass!' And the bride looked up at the glass, just in time to see the Captain cutting her head off; and he chopped her in pieces, and peppered her, and salted her, and put her in the pie, and sent it to the baker's, and ate it all, and picked the bones.

Captain Murderer went on in this way, prospering exceedingly, until he came to choose a bride from two twin sisters, and at first didn't know which to choose. For, though one was fair, and the other dark, they were both equally beautiful. But the fair twin loved him, and the dark twin hated him, so he chose the fair one. The dark twin would have prevented the marriage if she could, but she couldn't; however, on the night before it, much suspecting Captain Murderer, she stole out and climbed his garden wall, and looked in at his window through a chink in the shutter, and saw him having his teeth filed sharp. Next day she listened all day, and heard him make his joke about the house-lamb. And that day month he had the paste rolled out, and cut the fair twin's head off, and chopped her in pieces, and peppered her, and salted her, and put her in the pie, and sent it to the baker's, and ate it all, and picked the bones.

Now, the dark twin had had her suspicions much increased by the filing of the Captain's teeth, and again by the house-lamb joke. Putting all things together when he gave out that her sister was dead, she divined the truth, and determined to be revenged. So, she went up to Captain Murderer's house, and knocked at the knocker, and pulled at the bell, and, when the Captain came to the door, said: 'Dear Captain Murderer, marry me next, for I always loved you, and was jealous of my sister.' The Captain took it as a compliment, and made a polite answer, and the marriage was quickly arranged. On the night before it, the bride again climbed to his window, and again saw him having his teeth filed sharp. At this sight she laughed, such a terrible laugh at the chink in the shutter, that the Captain's blood curdled, and he said: 'I hope nothing has disagreed with me!' At that, she laughed again, a still more terrible laugh, and the shutter was opened and search made, but she was nimbly gone, and there was no one. Next day they went to church in a coach and twelve, and were married. And that day month she rolled the pie-crust out, and Captain Murderer cut her head off, and chopped her in pieces, and peppered her, and salted her, and put her in the pie, and sent it to the baker's, and ate it all, and picked the bones.

But, before she began to roll out the paste, she had taken a deadly poison of most awful character, distilled from toads' eyes and spiders' knees; and Captain Murderer had hardly picked her last bone, when he began to swell, and to turn blue, and to be all over spots, and to scream. And he went on swelling and turning bluer, and being more all over spots and screaming, until he reached from floor to ceiling, and from wall to wall; and then, at one o'clock in the morning, he blew up with a loud explosion. At the sound of it, all the milk-white horses in the stables broke their halters and went mad, and then they galloped over everybody in Captain Murderer's house (beginning with the family blacksmith who had filed his teeth) until the whole were dead, and then they galloped away.

Charles Dickens: *The Complete Ghost Stories*

MORE BREAKFASTS

A very special thing

Kipps made a very special thing of his breakfast. Daily once-hopeless dreams came true then. It had been customary in the Emporium to supplement Shalford's generous, indeed unlimited, supply of bread and butter-substitute by private purchases, and this had given Kipps very broad artistic conceptions of what the meal might be. Now there would be a cutlet or so or a mutton chop – this splendour Buggins had reported from the great London clubs – haddock, kipper, whiting, or fish-balls, eggs, boiled or scrambled, or eggs and bacon, kidney also frequently, and sometimes liver. Amidst a garland of such themes, sausages, black and white puddings, bubble-and-squeak, fried cabbage and scallops, came and went. Always as camp followers came potted meat in all varieties, cold bacon, German sausage, brawn, marmalade, and two sorts of jam; and when he had finished these he would sit among his plates and smoke a cigarette, and look at all these dishes crowded round him with beatific approval. It was his principal meal.

H. G. Wells: *Kipps*

Breakfast at Plumstead Episcopi

And now let us observe the well-furnished breakfast-parlour at Plumstead Episcopi, and the comfortable air of all the belongings of the rectory. Comfortable they certainly were, but neither gorgeous nor even grand; indeed, considering the money that had been spent there, the eye and taste might have been better served; there was an air of heaviness about the rooms which might have been avoided without any sacrifice of propriety; colours might have been better chosen and lights more perfectly diffused; but perhaps in doing so the thorough clerical aspect of the whole might have been somewhat marred. At any rate, it was not without ample consideration that those thick, dark, costly carpets were put down; those embossed, but sombre papers hung up; those heavy curtains draped so as to half exclude the light of the sun. Nor were these old-fashioned chairs, bought at a price far exceeding that now given for more modern goods, without a purpose. The breakfast-service on the table was equally costly and equally plain. The apparent object had been to spend money without obtaining a brilliancy or splendour. The urn was of thick and solid silver, as were also the tea-pot, coffee-pot, cream-ewer, and sugar-bowl; the cups were old, dim dragon china, worth about a pound a piece, but very despicable in the eyes of the uninitiated. The silver forks were so heavy as to be disagreeable to the hand, and the bread-basket was of a weight really formidable to any but robust persons. The tea consumed was the very best, the coffee the very blackest, the cream the very thickest; there was dry toast and buttered toast, muffins and crumpets; hot bread and cold bread, white bread and brown bread, home-made bread and bakers' bread, wheaten bread and oaten bread; and if there be other breads than these, they were there; there were eggs in napkins, and crispy bits of bacon under silver covers; and there were little fishes in a little box, and devilled kidneys frizzling on a hot-water dish; – which, by-the-by, were placed closely contiguous to the plate of the worthy archdeacon himself. Over and above this, on a snow white napkin, spread upon the sideboard, was a huge ham and a huge sirloin; the latter having laden the dinner table on the previous evening. Such was the ordinary fare at Plumstead Episcopi.

Anthony Trollope: *The Warden*

Coffee and burgoo

Hornblower went below to where Polwheal had his breakfast awaiting him.

'Coffee, sir,' said Polwheal. 'Burgoo.'

Hornblower sat down at table; in the seven months' voyage every luxury had long since been consumed. The coffee was a black extract of burnt bread, and all that could be said in its favour was that it was sweet and hot. The burgoo was a savoury mess of unspeakable appearance compounded of mashed biscuit crumbs and minced salt beef. Hornblower ate absentmindedly. With his left hand he tapped a biscuit on the table so that the weevils would all be induced to have left it by the time he had finished his burgoo.

There were ship-noises all round him as he ate. Every time the *Lydia* rolled and pitched a trifle as she reached the crest of the swell which was lifting her, the woodwork all creaked gently in unison. Overhead came the sound of Gerard's shod feet as he paced the quarterdeck, and sometimes the pattering of horny bare feet as some member of the crew trotted by. From forward came a monotonous steady clanking as the pumps were put to the daily task of pumping out the ship's bilge. But these noises were all transient and interrupted; there was one sound which went on all the time so steadily that the ear grew accustomed to it and noticed it only when the attention was specially directed to it – the sound of the breeze in the innumerable ropes of the rigging. It was just the faintest singing, a harmony of a thousand high-pitched tones and overtones, but it could be heard in every part of the ship, transmitted from the chains through the timbers along with the slow, periodic creaking.

Hornblower finished his burgoo, and was turning his attention to the biscuit he had been rapping on the table. He contemplated it with calm disfavour; it was poor food for a man, and in the absence of butter – the last cask had gone rancid a month back – he would have to wash down the dry mouthfuls with sips of burnt-bread coffee. But before he could take his first bite a wild cry from above caused him to sit still with the biscuit half-way to his mouth.

'Land ho!' he heard. 'Deck there! Land two points on the larboard bow, sir.'

C. S. Forester: *The Happy Return*

A snood of coarse porridge

In the large kitchen, which occupied most of the middle of the house, a sullen fire burned, the smoke of which wavered up the blackened walls and over the deal table, darkened by age and dirt, which was roughly set for a meal. A snood full of coarse porridge hung over the fire, and standing with one arm resting upon the high mantel, looking moodily down into the heaving contents of the snood, was a tall young man whose riding-boots were splashed with mud to the thigh, and whose coarse linen shirt was open to his waist. The firelight lit up his diaphragm muscles as they heaved slowly in rough rhythm with the porridge.

He looked up as Judith entered, and gave a short, defiant laugh, but said nothing. Judith crossed slowly over until she stood by his side. She was as tall as he. They stood in silence, she staring at him, and he down into the secret crevasses of the porridge.

'Well, mother mine,' he said at last, 'here I am, you see. I said I would be in time for breakfast, and I have kept my word.'

His voice had a low, throaty, animal quality, a sneering warmth that wound a velvet ribbon of sexuality over the outward coarseness of the man.

Judith's breath came in long shudders. She thrust her arms deeper into her shawl. The porridge gave an ominous leering heave; it might almost have been endowed with life, so uncannily did its movements keep pace with the human passions that throbbed above it.

'Cur,' said Judith, levelly, at last. 'Coward! Liar! Libertine! Who were you with last night? Moll at the mill or Violet at the vicarage? Or Ivy, perhaps, at the ironmongery? Seth – my son . . .' Her deep, dry voice quivered, but she whipped it back, and her next words flew out at him like a lash.

'Do you want to break my heart?'

'Yes,' said Seth, with an elemental simplicity.

The porridge boiled over.

Judith knelt, and hastily and absently ladled it off the floor back into the snood, biting back her tears. While she was thus engaged, there was a confused blur of voices and boots in the yard outside. The men were coming in to breakfast.

Stella Gibbons: *Cold Comfort Farm*

Chai with moloko

So now, this smiling winter morning, I drink this very strong chai with moloko and spoon after spoon after spoon of sugar, me having a sladky tooth, and I dragged out of the oven the breakfast my poor old mum had cooked for me. It was an egg fried, that and no more, but I made toast and ate egg and toast and jam, smacking away at it while I read the gazetta. The gazetta was the usual about ultra-violence and bank robberies and strikes and footballers making everybody paralytic with fright by threatening to not play next Saturday if they did not get higher wages, naughty malchickiwicks as they were. Also there were more space-trips and bigger stereo TV screens and offers of free packets of soapflakes in exchange for the labels on soup-tins, amazing offer for one week only, which made me smeck. And there was a bolshy big article on Modern Youth (meaning me, so I gave the old bow, grinning like bezoomny) by some very clever bald chelloveck. I read this with care, my brothers, slurping away at the old chai, cup after tass after chasha, crunching my lomticks of black toast dipped in jammiwam and eggiweg. This learned veck said the usual veshches, about no parental discipline, as he called it, and the shortage of real horrorshow teachers who would lambast bloody beggary out of their innocent poops and make them go boohoohoo for mercy. All this was gloopy and made me smeck, but it was like nice to go on knowing one was making the news all the time, O my brothers. Every day there was something about Modern Youth, but the vest veshch they ever had in the old gazetta was by some starry pop in a doggy collar who said that in his considered opinion and he was govoreeting as a man of Bog IT WAS THE DEVIL THAT WAS ABROAD and was like ferreting his way into like young innocent flesh, and it was the adult world that could take the responsibility for this with their wars and bombs and nonsense. So that was all right. So he knew what he talked of, being a Godman. So we young innnocent malchicks could take no blame. Right right right.

Anthony Burgess: *A Clockwork Orange*

THE GREAT OUTDOORS

Fresh fish for breakfast

They came back to camp wonderfully refreshed, glad-hearted, and ravenous; and they soon had the camp-fire blazing up again. Huck found a spring of clear water close by, and the boys made cups of broad oak or hickory leaves, and felt that water, sweetened with such a wild-wood charm as that, would be a good enough substitute for coffee. While Joe was slicing bacon for breakfast, Tom and Huck asked him to hold on a minute; they stepped to a promising nook in the river bank and threw in their lines; almost immediately they had reward. Joe had not had time to get impatient before they were back again with some handsome bass, a couple of sun-perch, and a small cat-fish – provision enough for quite a family. They fried the fish with the bacon and were astonished; for no fish had ever seemed so delicious before. They did not know that the quicker a freshwater fish is on the fire after he is caught the better he is; and they reflected little upon what a sauce open-air sleeping, open-air exercise, bathing, and a large ingredient of hunger make, too.

Mark Twain: *The Adventures of Tom Sawyer*

Big Two-Hearted River

Nick was hungry. He did not believe he had ever been hungrier. He opened and emptied a can of pork and beans and a can of spaghetti into the frying-pan.

'I've got a right to eat this kind of stuff, if I'm willing to carry it,'

Nick said. His voice sounded strange in the darkening woods. He did not speak again.

He started a fire with some chunks of pine he got with the axe from a stump. Over the fire he stuck a wire grill, pushing the four legs down into the ground with his boot. Nick put the frying-pan on the grill over flames. He was hungrier. The beans and spaghetti warmed. Nick stirred them and mixed them together. They began to bubble, making little bubbles that rose with difficulty to the surface. There was a good smell. Nick got out a bottle of tomato ketchup and cut four slices of bread. The little bubbles were coming faster now. Nick sat down beside the fire and lifted the frying-pan off. He poured about half the contents out into the tin plate. It spread slowly on the plate. Nick knew it was too hot. He poured on some tomato ketchup. He knew the beans and spaghetti were still too hot. He looked at the fire, then at the tent, he was not going to spoil it all by burning his tongue. For years he had never enjoyed fried bananas because he had never been able to wait for them to cool. His tongue was very sensitive. He was very hungry. Across the river in the swamp, in the almost dark, he saw a mist rising. He looked at the tent once more. All right. He took a full spoonful from the plate.

'Chrise,' Nick said, 'Geezus Chrise,' he said happily.

He ate the whole plateful before he remembered the bread. Nick finished the second plateful with the bread, mopping the plate shiny. He had not eaten since a cup of coffee and a ham sandwich in the station restaurant at St Ignace. It had been a very fine experience. He had been that hungry before, but had not been able to satisfy it. He could have made camp hours before if he had wanted to. There were plenty of good places to camp on the river. But this was good.

Nick tucked two big chips of pine under the grill. The fire flared up. He had forgotten to get water for the coffee. Out of the pack he got a folding canvas bucket and walked down the hill, across the edge of the meadow, to the stream. The other bank was in the white mist. The grass was wet and cold as he knelt on the bank and dipped the canvas bucket into the stream. It bellied and pulled hard in the current. The water was ice cold. Nick rinsed the bucket and carried it full up to the camp. Up away from the stream it was not so cold.

Nick drove another big nail and hung up the bucket full of water. He dipped the coffee pot half full, put some more chips under the grill on to the fire and put the pot on. He could not remember which way he made coffee. He could remember an argument about it with Hopkins, but not which side he had taken. He decided to bring it to a boil. He remembered now that was Hopkins's way. He had once argued about everything with Hopkins. While he waited for the coffee to boil, he opened a small can of apricots. He liked to open cans. He emptied the can of apricots out into a tin cup. While he watched the coffee on the fire, he drank the juice syrup of the apricots, carefully at first to keep from spilling, then meditatively, sucking the apricots down. They were better than fresh apricots.

The coffee boiled as he watched. The lid came up and coffee and grounds ran down the side of the pot. Nick took it off the grill. It was a triumph for Hopkins. He put sugar in the empty apricot cup and poured some of the coffee out to cool. It was too hot to pour and he used his hat to hold the handle of the coffee pot. He would not let it steep in the pot at all. Not the first cup. It should be straight Hopkins all the way. Hop deserved that. He was a very serious coffee maker. He was the most serious man Nick had ever known. Not heavy, serious. That was a long time ago. Hopkins spoke without moving his lips. He had played polo. He made millions of dollars in Texas. He had borrowed car fare to go to Chicago, when the wire came that his first big well had come in. He could have wired for money. That would have been too slow. They called Hop's girl the Blonde Venus. Hop did not mind because she was not his real girl. Hopkins said very confidently that none of them would make fun of his real girl. He was right. Hopkins went away when the telegram came. That was on the Black River. It took eight days for the telegram to reach him. Hopkins gave away his .22 calibre Colt automatic pistol to Nick. He gave his camera to Bill. It was to remember him always by. They were all going fishing again next summer. The Hop Head was rich. He would get a yacht and they would all cruise along the north shore of Lake Superior. He was excited but serious. They said good-bye and all felt bad. It broke up the trip. They never saw Hopkins again. That was a long time ago on the Black River.

Nick drank his coffee according to Hopkins. The coffee was bitter. Nick laughed. It made a good ending to the story.

Ernest Hemingway: *In Our Time*

Irish stew

It was still early when we got settled, and George said that, as we had plenty of time, it would be a splendid opportunity to try a good slap-up supper. He said he would show us what could be done up the river in the way of cooking, and suggested that, with the vegetables and the remains of the cold beef and general odds and ends, we should make an Irish stew.

It seemed a fascinating idea. George gathered wood and made a fire, and Harris and I started to peel the potatoes. I should never have thought that peeling potatoes was such an undertaking. The job turned out to be the biggest thing of its kind that I had ever been in. We began cheerfully, one might almost say skittishly, but our lightheartedness was gone by the time the first potato was finished. The more we peeled, the more peel there seemed to be left on; by the time we had got all the peel off and all the eyes out, there was no potato left – at least none worth speaking of. George came and had a look at it – it was about the size of a pea-nut, He said:

'Oh, that won't do! You're wasting them. You must scrape them.'

So we scraped them, and that was harder work than peeling. They are such an extraordinary shape, potatoes – all bumps and warts and hollows. We worked steadily for five-and-twenty minutes, and did four potatoes. Then we struck. We said we should require the rest of the evening for scraping ourselves.

I never saw such a thing as potato-scraping for making a fellow in a mess. It seemed difficult to believe that the potato-scrapings in which Harris and I stood half-smothered, could have come off four potatoes. It shows you what can be done with economy and care.

George said it was absurd to have only four potatoes in an Irish stew, so we washed half a dozen or so more, and put them in without peeling. We also put in a cabbage and about half a peck of peas. George stirred it all up, and then he said that there seemed to be a lot of room to spare, so we overhauled both the hampers, and picked out all the odds and ends and the remnants, and added them to the stew. There were half a pork pie and a bit of cold boiled bacon left, and we put them in. Then George found half a tin of potted salmon, and he emptied that into the pot.

He said that was the advantage of Irish stew: you got rid of such a lot of things. I fished out a couple of eggs that had got cracked, and we put those in. George said they would thicken the gravy.

I forget the other ingredients, but I know nothing was wasted; and I remember that, towards the end, Montmorency, who had evinced great interest in the proceedings throughout, strolled away with an earnest and thoughtful air, reappearing, a few minutes afterwards, with a dead water-rat in his mouth, which he evidently wished to present as his contribution to the dinner; whether in a sarcastic spirit, or with a genuine desire to assist, I cannot say.

We had a discussion as to whether the rat should go in or not. Harris said that he thought it would be all right, mixed up with the other things, and that every little helped; but George stood up for precedent. He said he had never heard of water-rats in Irish stew, and he would rather be on the safe side, and not try experiments.

Harris said:

'If you never try a new thing, how can you tell what it's like? It's men such as you that hamper the world's progress. Think of the man who first tried German sausage!'

It was a great success, that Irish stew. I don't think I ever enjoyed a meal more. There was something so fresh and piquant about it. One's palate gets so tired of the old hackneyed things: here was a dish with a new flavour, with a taste like nothing else on earth.

And it was nourishing, too. As George said, there was good stuff in it. The peas and potatoes might have been a bit softer, but we all had good teeth, so that did not matter much; and as for the gravy, it was a poem – a little too rich, perhaps, for a weak stomach, but nutritious.

We finished up with tea and cherry tart. Montmorency had a fight with the kettle during tea-time, and came off a poor second.

Jerome K. Jerome: *Three Men in a Boat*

Herbs and stewed rabbit

Gollum returned quietly and peered over Sam's shoulder. Looking at Frodo, he shut his eyes and crawled away without a sound. Sam came to him a moment later and found him chewing something and muttering to himself. On the ground beside him lay two small rabbits, which he was beginning to eye greedily.

'Sméagol always helps,' he said. 'He has brought rabbits, nice rabbits. But master has gone to sleep, and perhaps Sam wants to sleep. Doesn't want rabbits now? Sméagol tries to help, but he can't catch things all in a minute.'

Sam, however, had no objection to rabbit at all, and said so. At least not to cooked rabbit. All hobbits, of course, can cook, for they begin to learn the art before their letters (which many never reach); but Sam was a good cook, even by hobbit reckoning, and he had done a good deal of the camp-cooking on their travels, when there was a chance. He still hopefully carried some of his gear in his pack: a small tinder-box, two small shallow pans, the smaller fitting into the larger; inside them a wooden spoon, a short two-pronged fork and some skewers were stowed; and hidden at the bottom of the pack in a flat wooden box a dwindling treasure, some salt. But he needed a fire, and other things besides. He thought for a bit, while he took out his knife, cleaned and whetted it, and began to dress the rabbits. He was not going to leave Frodo alone asleep even for a few minutes.

'Now, Gollum,' he said, 'I've another job for you. Go and fill these pans with water, and bring 'em back!'

'Sméagol will fetch water, yes,' said Gollum. 'But what does the hobbit want all that water for? He has drunk, he has washed.'

'Never you mind,' said Sam. 'If you can't guess, you'll soon find out. And the sooner you fetch the water, the sooner you'll learn. Don't you damage one of my pans, or I'll carve you into mince-meat.'

While Gollum was away Sam took another look at Frodo. He was still sleeping quietly, but Sam was now struck most by the leanness of his face and hands. 'Too thin and drawn he is,' he muttered. 'Not right for a hobbit. If I can get these coneys cooked, I'm going to wake him up.'

Sam gathered a pile of the driest fern, and then scrambled up the bank collecting a bundle of twigs and broken wood; the fallen branch of a cedar at the top gave him a good supply. He cut out some turves at the foot of the bank just outside the fern-brake, and made a shallow hole and laid his fuel in it. Being handy with flint and tinder he soon had a small blaze going. It made little or no smoke but gave off an aromatic scent. He was just stooping over his fire, shielding it and building it up with heavier wood, when Gollum returned, carrying the pans carefully and grumbling to himself.

He set the pans down, and then suddenly saw what Sam was doing. He gave a thin hissing shriek, and seemed to be both frightened and angry. 'Ach! Sss – no!' he cried. 'No! Silly hobbits, foolish, yes foolish! They mustn't do it!'

'Mustn't do what?' asked Sam in surprise.

'Not make the nassty red tongues,' hissed Gollum. 'Fire, fire! It's dangerous, yes it is. It burns, it kills. And it will bring enemies, yes it will.'

'I don't think so,' said Sam. 'Don't see why it should, if you don't put wet stuff on it and make a smother. But if it does, it does. I'm going to risk it, anyhow. I'm going to stew these coneys.'

'Stew the rabbits!' squealed Gollum in dismay. 'Spoil beautiful meat Sméagol saved for you, poor hungry Sméagol! What for? What for, silly hobbit? They are young, they are tender, they are nice. Eat them, eat them!' He clawed at the nearest rabbit, already skinned and lying by the fire.

'Now, now!' said Sam. 'Each to his own fashion. Our bread chokes you, and raw coney chokes me. If you give me a coney, the coney's mine, see, to cook, if I have a mind. And I have. You needn't watch me. Go and catch another and eat it as you fancy – somewhere private and out o' my sight. Then you won't see the fire, and I shan't see you, and we'll both be the happier. I'll see the fire don't smoke, if that's any comfort to you.'

Gollum withdrew grumbling, and crawled into the fern. Sam busied himself with his pans. 'What a hobbit needs with coney,' he said to himself, 'is some herbs and roots, especially taters – not to mention bread. Herbs we can manage, seemingly.'

'Gollum!' he called softly. 'Third time pays for all. I want some herbs.' Gollum's head peeped out of the fern, but his looks were neither helpful nor friendly. 'A few bay-leaves, some thyme and sage, will do – before the water boils,' said Sam.

'No!' said Gollum. 'Sméagol is not pleased. And Sméagol doesn't like smelly leaves. He doesn't eat grasses or roots, no precious, not till he's starving or very sick, poor Sméagol.'

'Sméagol'll get into real hot water, when this water boils, if he don't do as he's asked,' growled Sam. 'Sam'll put his head in it, yes precious. And I'd make him look for turnips and carrots, and taters too, if it was the time o' the year. I'll bet there's all sorts of good things running wild in this country. I'd give a lot for half a dozen taters.'

'Sméagol won't go, O no precious, not this time,' hissed Gollum. 'He's frightened, and he's very tired, and this hobbit's not nice, not nice at all. Sméagol won't grub for roots and carrotses and – taters. What's taters, precious, eh, what's taters?'

'Po-ta-toes,' said Sam. 'The Gaffer's delight, and rare good ballast for an empty belly. But you won't find any, so you needn't look. But be good Sméagol and fetch me the herbs, and I'll think better of you. What's more, if you turn over a new leaf, and keep it turned, I'll cook you some taters one of these days. I will: fried fish and chips served by S. Gamgee. You couldn't say no to that.'

'Yes, yes we could. Spoiling nice fish, scorching it. Give me fish *now*, and keep nassty chips!'

'Oh you're hopeless,' said Sam. 'Go to sleep!'

In the end he had to find what he wanted for himself; but he did not have to go far, not out of sight of the place where his master lay, still sleeping. For a while Sam sat musing, and tending the fire till the water boiled. The daylight grew and the air became warm; the dew faded off turf and leaf. Soon the rabbits cut up lay simmering in their pans with the bunched herbs. Almost Sam fell asleep as the time went by. He let them stew for close on an hour, testing them now and again with his fork, and tasting the broth.

When he thought all was ready he lifted the pans off the fire, and crept along to Frodo. Frodo half opened his eyes as Sam stood over him, and then he wakened from his dreaming: another gentle, unrecoverable dream of peace.

'Hullo, Sam!' he said. 'Not resting? Is anything wrong? What is the time?'

'About a couple of hours after daybreak,' said Sam, 'and nigh on half past eight by Shire clocks, maybe. But nothing's wrong. Though it ain't quite what I'd call right: no stock, no onions, no taters. I've got a bit of a stew for you, and some broth, Mr Frodo. Do you good. You'll have to sup it in your mug; or straight from the pan, when it's cooled a bit. I haven't brought no bowls, nor nothing proper.'

Frodo yawned and stretched. 'You should have been resting, Sam,' he said. 'And lighting a fire was dangerous in these parts. But I do feel hungry. Hmm! Can I smell it from here? What have you stewed?'

'A present from Sméagol,' said Sam: 'A brace o' young coneys; though I fancy Gollum's regretting them now. But there's nought to go with them but a few herbs.'

Sam and his master sat just within the fern-brake and ate their stew from the pans, sharing the old fork and spoon. They allowed themselves half a piece of the Elvish waybread each. It seemed a feast.

'Wheew! Gollum!' Sam called and whistled softly. 'Come on! Still time to change your mind. There's some left, if you want to try stewed coney.' There was no answer.

'Oh well, I suppose he's gone off to find something for himself. We'll finish it,' said Sam.

'And then you must take some sleep,' said Frodo.

'Don't you drop off, while I'm nodding, Mr Frodo. I don't feel too sure of him. There's a good deal of Stinker – the bad Gollum, if you understand me – in him still, and it's getting stronger again. Not but what I think he'd try to throttle me first now. We don't see eye to eye, and he's not pleased with Sam, O no precious, not pleased at all.'

J. R. R. Tolkien: *The Two Towers*

REGIONAL VARIETY

Down south t' women doesn't bake

'Pass me up them inch nails, Joe,' said Mr Oakroyd. Then he reflected a minute or two. 'Well, I must say I've seen better cooking i' my time than you get round these parts. That's because you're out o' Yorkshire. Down south here t'women doesn't bake and you can't get a curran' teacake or a flat cake or a fatty cake or owt like that. Eh, I'd a right good laugh yesterda'. Woman where I am – Mrs Cullin her name is – she's a widow woman – her husband were at gas-works here and had a good job too, she tells me – she's a decent clean little body, and friendly like – she tells me all sorts – well, Mrs Cullin, she says to me yesterda', she says, "Now, Mr Oakroyd, I'm going to give you a treat," she says. "I've a joint o' beef for your dinner and you're a Yorkshireman, so I'm going to give you some Yorkshire pudding with it," she says. In comes my dinner – bit o' beef, cabbage, potaters. I looks at it and says "Here, Mrs Cullin, what about that Yorkshire pudding?" I says. "Let's have that first." She stares. "It's here," she says, pointing to t'plate. "What!" I says. "You don't mean this bit o' custard, soft batter stuff, under t'cabbage?" "Yes, I do," she says. "If that isn't Yorkshire pudding, what is it?" "Nay," I says, "you mun't ask me, Missis, what it is. All I knaw is, it's no more Yorkshire pudding ner I am. It's a bit o' custard or pancake, likely enough." And then I tells her about Yorkshire pudding. And tak' notice o' this, Joe, 'cos it'll happen come in handy some time.' Mr Oakroyd paused to relight his pipe, blew out a cloud or two of *Old Salt*, then continued.

'"To begin wi'," I says, "a Yorkshire pudding is eaten by itsen and not mixed up wi' meat and potaters, all in a mush. And it comes straight out o' t'oven," I says, "straight on to t'plate. No waiting," I says, "or you'll spoil it. If you don't put it straight on to t'plate you might as well go and sole your boots with it. And another thing," I says, "you've got to have your oven hot, I do knaw that. Then if you've mixed right and your oven's hot, pudding'll come out as light as a feather, crisp and brarn, just a top and a bottom, you might say, wi' none o' this custardy stuff in t'middle. Nah d'you see, Missis?" I says. "Nay," she says, "I can't learn all that at my time o' life, and you're letting your dinner get cold wi' talking about your hot ovens," she says. And then we'd a right good laugh together, and I heard her telling her daughter – she's in a draper's – all about it last night. She has this lass at home and a lad, and another lad away i' t'Navy, and they're all courting – even t'sailor's young woman is allus coming in – so we see a bit o' company. And they're all coming o' Saturday night to see us.'

J. B. Priestley: *The Good Companions*

Bourgeoisburger with onions

I climb out of the Kaiser and walk across the parking lot and in the side door of the EMPEROR'S FEAST and am surprised to see Tsvkzov's not there yet. The place's pretty deserted as it usually is at this hour but of all things seat thirty-eight on the seventy-two stool EMPEROR'S FEAST HAMBURGER BAR is occupied by one of these teenage girls that looks like an unfinished construction project.

'Okay sweetie,' I say, 'move it off the stool, it's my seat.'

She turns around and looks at me with a pair of sunglasses so dark it's a wonder she knows which way to look and takes a piece of unchewed hamburger out of her mouth with her fingers and drops it right on my left shoe, the juvenile delinquent.

'Huh?' she says.

'I say you're on my stool.'

'Look Grampa nobody's sitting in the other fifty stools that I can see,' she says so I guess she can see.

'That may be sweetie but I own this place and I always sit on stool thirty-eight.'

'You own this place?' she says sort of wiggling her wrist.

'That's what I said.'

'Oh. Well maybe you can do something about these hamburgers. They taste like dead cat.'

As a matter of fact we don't use cats in our hamburger most of the time but I can't give her the news because she stomps off and out the door which I don't give a damn about because here you've got to pay before you eat. I hoist myself up on the stool and run through the menu which is printed in the formica counter in front of each stool. As far as I can tell from the remains, the little snot was eating a PEASANTBURGER which is the cheapest and weighs a tenth of a pound raw. After that comes the BOURGEOISBURGER at an eighth of a pound and then the DUKEBURGER at a fourth-pound and next the KINGBURGER at a half-pound and the CZARBURGER at a full pound and then the EMPERORBURGER running at two full pounds. Lastly we have at four full pounds the GODBURGER which of course we don't put on the menu. All of these burgers have different size buns and different size onions and tomatoes and lettuce pieces, though the PEASANTBURGER consists of only a half-bun and a meat pattie and a tenth of an ounce of mustard in a little plastic cup, and it doesn't come with utensils so the PEASANTBURGER eater always has to ask for utensils and water and most often he asks for a knife to get the mustard out of the little plastic cup as it cannot be otherwise got out without making a big mess. And if he doesn't use the mustard, it just adds to our profit.

After a minute one of the guys behind the counter dressed up as a court dandy comes up and takes my order which is a BOURGEOIS-BURGER with lots of onions, and he runs off and gets one and brings it right back. I get a glass of water with that and now all I'm mising is Tsvkzov and wonder why he's late. Three teenage couples come in the door and wobble over to one of the tables and it's pretty clear what they're here for, we've got that too.

I run through my BOURGEOISBURGER pretty damn fast because though it looks big it's the geometric pattern on the plate that does that and it's really pretty damn small, and not too many people order this one because they can't pronounce it which shoves them up to the DUKEBURGER and KINGBURGER class which is where we really begin to make money. So anyway I'm still a bit hungry and whistle for the boy and order a dish of EMPEROR'S ICE CREAM, KINGSIZE, and he brings that.

Just then Tsvkzov whips in the side door and trots across the hamburger pattern carpet and plunks himself down on the stool next to mine.

'Hi Tsvkzov, I've got some hot stuff for you.'

'How hot?'

'Damn hot. Sweating hot,' I say.

'Too hot?'

'Not if you play it cool.'

Stanley Crawford: *Gascoyne*

Nouvelle cuisine

For supper Jill cooks a filet of sole, lemony, light, simmered in sunshine, skin flaky brown; Nelson gets a hamburger with wheatgerm sprinkled on it to remind him of a Nutburger. Wheatgerm, zucchini, water chestnuts, celery salt, Familia: these are some of the exotic items Jill's shopping brings into the house. Her cooking tastes to him of things he never had: candlelight, saltwater, health fads, wealth, class. Jill's family had a servant, and it takes her some nights to understand that dirtied dishes do not clear and clean themselves by magic, but have to be carried and washed. Rabbit, still, Saturday mornings, is the one to vacuum the rooms, to bundle his shirts and the sheets for the laundry, to sort out Nelson's socks and underwear for the washer in the basement. He can see, what these children cannot, dust accumulate, deterioration advance, chaos seep in, time conquer. But for her cooking he is willing to be her servant, part-time. Her cooking has renewed his taste for life. They have wine now with supper, a California white in a half-gallon jug. And always a salad: salad in Brewer County cuisine tends to be a brother of sauerkraut, fat with creamy dressing, but Jill's hands toss lettuce in a glowing film invisible as health. Where Janice would for dessert offer some doughy goodie from the Half-A-Loaf, Jill concocts designs of fruit. And her coffee is black nectar compared to the watery tar Janice used to serve. Contentment makes Harry motionless;

he watches the dishes be skimmed from the table, and resettles expansively in the living room. When the dishwashing machine is fed and chugging contentedly, Jill comes into the living room, sits on the tacky carpet, and plays the guitar.

John Updike: *Rabbit Redux*

Claret with a greyish tinge

The half-past six o'clock dinner came all too swiftly. Glared upon by an unshaded lamp that sat like a ball of fire in the centre of the table, we laboured in the trough of a sea of the thickest ox-tail soup; a large salmon followed; with the edge of dubious appetite already turned, we saw the succeeding items of the menu spread forth on the table like a dummy hand at bridge. The boiled turkey, with its satellite ham, the roast saddle of mutton, with its stable companion the stack of cutlets; the succeeding course, where a team of four wild duck struggled for the lead with an open tart and a sago pudding. Like Agag, we went delicately, and, like Agag, it availed us nothing.

I watched my *vis-à-vis*, little Mrs Flurry, furtively burying a slab of turkey beneath mashed potatoes as neatly as a little dog buries a bone; her green kitten's eyes met mine without a change of expression, and turned to her glass, which Colonel Newcome had filled with claret. 'The beaded bubbles, winking at the brim,' had a greyish tinge.

'Cousin Lucius!' observed Mrs Flurry, in a silence that presently happened to fall, 'can you remember who painted that picture of our great-grandfather – the one over the door I mean?'

Mr Butler-Knox, a small, grey-bearded, elderly gentleman, wholly, up to the present, immersed in carving, removed the steam of the ducks from his eye-glasses, and concentrated them upon the picture.

'It's by Maclise, isn't it?' went on Sally, leaning forward to get a nearer view.

In that moment, when all heads turned to the picture, I plainly saw her draw the glass of claret to the verge of the table, it disappeared beneath it and returned to its place empty. Almost simultaneously, the black-and-tan terrior sprang from a lair near my feet, and hurried from the room, shaking his ears vigorously. Mrs Flurry's eyes wavered from the portrait to mine, and her face became slowly and evenly pink, like an after-glow.

Somerville and Ross: *Further Experiences of an Irish R.M.*

WATCHING THE WAISTLINE

The strain of ideal living

Well might poor Robert remember the devastation of his home when Daisy, after the perusal of a little pamphlet which she picked up on a book-stall called *The Uric Acid Monthly*, came to the shattering conclusion that her buxom frame consisted almost entirely of waste-products which must be eliminated. For a greedy man the situation was frankly intolerable, for when he continued his ordinary diet (this was before the cursed advent of the Christian Science cook) she kept pointing to his well-furnished plate, and told him that every atom of that beef or mutton and potatoes turned from the moment he swallowed it into chromagens and toxins, and that his apparent appetite was merely the result of fermentation. For herself, her platter was an abominable mess of cheese and proteid-powder, and apples and salad-oil, while round her, like saucers of specimen seeds, were ranged little piles of nuts and pine-kernels, which supplied body-building material, and which she weighed out with scrupulous accuracy, in accordance with the directions of *The Uric Acid Monthly*. Tea and coffee were taboo, since they flooded the blood with poisons, and the kitchen boiler rumbled day and night to supply the rivers of boiling water with which (taken in sips) she inundated her system. Strange gaunt females used to come down from London, with small parcels full of tough food that tasted of travelling-bags, and contained so much nutrition that quite a few pounds of it would furnish the daily rations of an army. Luckily even her iron constitution could not stand the strain of such ideal living for long, and her growing anæmia threatened to undermine a constitution seriously impaired by the precepts of perfect health. A course of beef-steaks and other substantial viands loaded with uric acid restored her to her former vigour.

E. F. Benson: *Queen Lucia*

More than flesh and blood can stand

She changed into her one-piece bathing-suit, put on her espadrilles
and a man's dressing-gown (no nonsense about it), and went to Eden
Roc. There was still time for a bathe before luncheon. She passed
through the Monkey House, looking about her to say good morning
to anyone she knew, for she felt on a sudden at peace with mankind,
and then stopped dead still. She could not believe her eyes. Beatrice
was sitting at one of the tables, by herself; she wore the pyjamas she
had bought at Molyneux's a day or two before, she had a string of
pearls round her neck, and Frank's quick eyes saw that she had just
had her hair waved; her cheeks, her eyes, her lips were made up. Fat,
nay vast, as she was, none could deny that she was an extremely
handsome woman. But what was she doing? With the slouching gait
of the Neanderthal man which was Frank's characteristic walk she
went up to Beatrice. In her black bathing-dress Frank looked like the
huge cetacean which the Japanese catch in the Torres Straits and
which the vulgar call a sea-cow.

'Beatrice, what are you doing?' she cried in her deep voice.

It was like the roll of thunder in the distant mountains. Beatrice
looked at her coolly.

'Eating,' she answered.

'Damn it, I can see you're eating.'

In front of Beatrice was a plate of *croissants* and a plate of butter, a
pot of strawberry jam, coffee, and a jug·of cream. Beatrice was
spreading butter thick on the delicious hot bread, covering this with
jam, and then pouring the thick cream over all.

'You'll kill yourself,' said Frank.

'I don't care,' mumbled Beatrice with her mouth full.

'You'll put on pounds and pounds.'

'Go to hell!'

She actually laughed in Frank's face. My God, how good those
croissants smelt!

'I'm disappointed in you, Beatrice. I thought you had more character.'

'It's your fault. That blasted woman. You would have her down.

For a fortnight I've watched her gorge like a hog. It's more than flesh and blood can stand. I'm going to have one square meal if I bust.'

The tears welled up to Frank's eyes. Suddenly she felt very weak and womanly. She would have liked a strong man to take her on his knee and pet her and cuddle her and call her little baby names. Speechless she sank down on a chair by Beatrice's side. A waiter came up. With a pathetic gesture she waved towards the coffee and *croissants*.

'I'll have the same,' she sighed.

She listlessly reached out her hand to take a roll, but Beatrice snatched away the plate.

'No, you don't,' she said. 'You wait till you get your own.'

Frank called her a name which ladies seldom apply to one another in affection. In a moment the waiter brought her *croissants*, butter, jam, and coffee.

'Where's the cream, you fool?' she roared like a lioness at bay.

She began to eat. She ate gluttonously. The place was beginning to fill up with bathers coming to enjoy a cocktail or two after having done their duty by the sun and the sea. Presently Arrow strolled along with Prince Roccamare. She had on a beautiful silk wrap which she held tightly round her with one hand in order to look as slim as possible and she bore her head high so that he should not see her double chin. She was laughing gaily. She felt like a girl. He had just told her (in Italian) that her eyes made the blue of the Mediterranean look like pea-soup. He left her to go into the men's room to brush his sleek black hair and they arranged to meet in five minutes for a drink. Arrow walked on to the women's room to put a little more rouge on her cheeks and a little more red on her lips. On her way she caught sight of Frank and Beatrice. She stopped. She could hardly believe her eyes.

'My God!' she cried. 'You beasts. You hogs.' She seized a chair. 'Waiter.'

Her appointment went clean out of her head. In the twinkling of an eye the waiter was at her side.

'Bring me what these ladies are having,' she ordered.

Frank lifted her great heavy head from her plate.

'Bring me some *pâté de foie gras*,' she boomed.

'Frank!' cried Beatrice.

'Shut up.'

'All right. I'll have some too.'

The coffee was brought and the hot rolls and cream and the *pâté de foie gras* and they set to. They spread the cream on the *pâté* and they ate it. They devoured great spoonfuls of jam. They crunched the delicious crisp bread voluptuously. What was love to Arrow then? Let the Prince keep his palace in Rome and his castle in the Apennines. They did not speak. What they were about was much too serious. They ate with solemn, ecstatic fervour.

'I haven't eaten potatoes for twenty-five years,' said Frank in a far-off brooding tone.

'Waiter,' cried Beatrice, 'bring fried potatoes for three.'

'*Très bien, Madame.*'

The potatoes were brought. Not all the perfumes of Arabia smelt so sweet. They ate them with their fingers.

'Bring me a dry Martini,' said Arrow.

'You can't have a dry Martini in the middle of a meal, Arrow,' said Frank.

'Can't I? You wait and see.'

'All right then. Bring me a double dry Martini,' said Frank.

'Bring three double dry Martinis,' said Beatrice.

They were brought and drunk at a gulp. The women looked at one another and sighed. The misunderstandings of the last fortnight dissolved and the sincere affection each had for the others welled up again in their hearts. They could hardly believe that they had ever contemplated the possibility of severing a friendship that had brought them so much solid satisfaction. They finished the potatoes.

'I wonder if they've got any chocolate éclairs,' said Beatrice.

'Of course they have.'

And of course they had. Frank thrust one whole into her huge mouth, swallowed it and seized another, but before she ate it she looked at the other two and plunged a vindictive dagger into the heart of the monstrous Lena.

'You can say what you like, but the truth is she played a damned rotten game of bridge, really.'

'Lousy,' agreed Arrow.

But Beatrice suddenly thought she would like a meringue.

W. Somerset Maugham: *The Three Fat Women of Antibes*

PIG

A papyrus from the pig

I began to understand that we were all to be covered with wreaths of lotus flowers, and that petals of roses would surround our new plates of alabaster, large and clear and milky-white, and I also understood that all of this, the girls, the flowers, the songs, and the intimacies of the servants – 'You are so beautiful,' whispered the serving girl to my mother even as her hip was being caressed, while my serving girl whispered to me, 'You are not old enough to know where I could kiss you!' – yes, these agreeable conversations (which I had heard at more than one feast) were not unusual, but tonight they offered a fine fever at just the moment when the pig was brought out to us by two black eunuchs, nude but for their cloths. Yet, tonight, these breechclouts had been studded with precious stones that could come only from the Pharaoh's linen. The male servants carried the body on a great black serving dish and set it in the center of our table in the midst of a quick movement by the dancing girls that had much beating of feet, much undulating of their bellies, and a scintillating play of notes from the three-string lyre, the sounds coming in all the quick multitude of some altercation between the birds in the Pharaoh's garden. I was now aware of animals crying out all over the place, a dog first.

Here was the pig. I was not ready for the sight. He looked alive and fierce and like a man. I had seen wild boars in their cage, and they were ugly and full of spiky hair matted with filth and litter. Their snouts made me think of the stumps of thieves' arms after the hands had been cut off or would have, if not for the two holes of the nostrils, as dull and stubborn as any two holes you could poke in the mud with your fingers. This pig, however, had had his hair shaved off, no, he was peeled, I saw, as I looked at him, and his under-skin, now nicely cooked, was pink. His two fangs were covered with gold leaf, his paws had been manicured, then fixed with silver leaf, his nose had been scraped, and painted pink, the buds of white flowers were in his nostrils, a pomegranate in his mouth, and the servants, revolving the platter to show all sides of this decorated beast to all of us, I was given a view of the spiral of his tail, yet before I could demonstrate my cleverness by commenting that the spiral reminded me of the snail, I was treated to another surprise; a small roll of papyrus had been inserted into the pig's well-scrubbed anus.

'It is for you to pluck it forth,' said Ptah-nem-hotep to Hathfertiti. With a sweet wash of giggles from the servants, full of the delight that they were witnessing the rarest of sights, Hathfertiti gave a kiss to her left hand, and with a flick of her fingertips plucked the papyrus from its place.

'What does it say?' asked Ptah-nem-hotep.

'I promise to read it before the meal is done,' Hathfertiti answered with a droll look, as though to give the papyrus time to breathe.

'No, read it now,' said our Pharaoh.

So she broke its seal of perfumed wax, unrolled it, gasped with delight as a ruby scarab fell into her plate – then touched it for luck to the tip of her nipple before she set it down. She read to all of us: 'Just a slave on the Night of the Pig, but may you seek My freedom,' to which my father and Menenhetet laughed. Ptah-nem-hotep and Hathfertiti did not. They stared back and forth with a tenderness so agreeable I wished to sit between them. It was as if there could be no end to the fascinating conversations they might have. All the while, my father looked on with pride, a happy, even a boyish look on his face as if by these attentions given to his wife, he was receiving an honour he had not wholly earned, while my great-grandfather kept a firm smile on his face until the corners of his mouth looked like two short fenceposts, and contented himself by rotating the great round black plate on which the pig rested, as though in this animal there were other messages to read.

Norman Mailer: *Ancient Evenings*

Pig

A dissertation upon roast pig

Of all the delicacies in the whole *mundus edibilis*, I will maintain it to be the most delicate – *princeps obsoniorum*.

I speak not of your grown porkers – things between pig and pork – those hobbydehoys – but a young and tender suckling – under a moon old – guiltless as yet of the sty – with no original speck of the *amor immunditiæ*, the hereditary failing of the first parent, yet manifest – his voice as yet not broken, but something between a childish treble, and a grumble – the mild forerunner or *præludium*, of a grunt.

He must be roasted. I am not ignorant that our ancestors ate them seethed or boiled – but what a sacrifice of the exterior tegument!

There is no flavour comparable, I will contend, to that of the crisp, tawny, well-watched, not over-roasted, *crackling*, as it is well called – the very teeth are invited to their share of the pleasure at this banquet in overcoming the coy, brittle resistance – with the adhesive oleaginous – O call it not fat – but an indefinable sweetness growing up to it – the tender blossoming of fat – fat cropped in the bud – taken in the shoot – in the first innocence – the cream and quintessence of the child-pig's yet pure food — the lean, no lean, but a kind of animal manna – or, rather, fat and lean (if it must be so) so blended and running into each other, that both together make but one ambrosian result, or common substance.

Behold him, while he is doing – it seemeth rather a refreshing warmth, than a scorching heat, that he is so passive to. How equably he twirleth round the string! – Now he is just done. To see the extreme sensibility of that tender age, he hath wept out his pretty eyes – radiant jellies – shooting stars –

See him in the dish, his second cradle, how meek he lieth! – wouldst thou have had this innocent grow up to the grossness and indocility which too often accompany maturer swinehood? Ten to one he would have proved a glutton, a sloven, an obstinate, disagreeable animal – wallowing in all manner of filthy conversation – from these sins he is happily snatched away –

Pig

Ere sin could blight, or sorrow fade,
Death came with timely care –

his memory is odoriferous – no clown curseth, while his stomach half rejecteth, the rank bacon – no coal-heaver bolteth him in reeking sausages – he hath a fair sepulchre in the grateful stomach of the judicious epicure – and for such a tomb might be content to die.

He is the best of Sapors. Pine-apple is great. She is indeed almost too transcendent – a delight, if not sinful, yet so like to sinning, that really a tender-conscienced person would do well to pause – too ravishing for mortal taste, she woundeth and excoriateth the lips that approach her – like lovers' kisses, she biteth – she is a pleasure bordering on pain from the fierceness and insanity of her relish – but she stoppeth at the palate – she meddleth not with the appetite – and the coarsest hunger might barter her consistently for a mutton chop.

Pig – let me speak his praise – is no less provocative of the appetite, than he is satisfactory to the criticalness of the censorious palate. The strong man may batten on him, and the weakling refuseth not his mild juices.

Unlike to mankind's mixed characters, a bundle of virtues and vices, inexplicably intertwisted, and not to be unravelled without hazard, he is – good throughout. No part of him is better or worse than another. He helpeth, as far as his little means extend, all around. He is the least envious of banquets. He is all neighbours' fare.

I am one of those, who freely and ungrudgingly impart a share of the good things of this life which fall to their lot (few as mine are in this kind) to a friend. I protest I take as great an interest in my friend's pleasures, his relishes, and proper satisfactions, as in mine own. 'Presents,' I often say, 'endear Absents.' Hares, pheasants, partridges, snipes, barn-door chickens (those 'tame villatic fowl'), capons, plovers, brawn, barrels of oysters, I dispense as freely as I receive them. I love to taste them, as it were, upon the tongue of my friend. But a stop must be put somewhere. One would not, like Lear, 'give every thing'. I make my stand upon pig.

Charles Lamb: *The Essays of Elia*

Pig

'All right. Light the fire.'

With some positive action before them, a little of the tension died. Ralph said no more, did nothing, stood looking down at the ashes round his feet. Jack was loud and active. He gave orders, sang, whistled, threw remarks at the silent Ralph – remarks that did not need an answer, and therefore could not invite a snub; and still Ralph was silent. No one, not even Jack, would ask him to move and in the end they had to build the fire three yards away and in a place not really as convenient. So Ralph asserted his chieftainship and could not have chosen a better way if he had thought for days. Against this weapon, so indefinable and so effective, Jack was powerless and raged without knowing why. By the time the pile was built, they were on different sides of a high barrier.

When they had dealt with the fire another crisis arose. Jack had no means of lighting it. Then to his surprise, Ralph went to Piggy and took the glasses from him. Not even Ralph knew how a link between him and Jack had been snapped and fastened elsewhere.

'I'll bring 'em back.'

'I'll come too.'

Piggy stood behind him, islanded in a sea of meaningless colour, while Ralph knelt and focused the glossy spot. Instantly the fire was alight Piggy held out his hands and grabbed the glasses back.

Before these fantastically attractive flowers of violet and red and yellow, unkindness melted away. They became a circle of boys round a camp fire and even Piggy and Ralph were half-drawn in. Soon some of the boys were rushing down the slope for more wood while Jack hacked the pig. They tried holding the whole carcass on a stake over the fire, but the stake burnt more quickly than the pig roasted. In the end they skewered bits of meat on branches and held them in the flames: and even then almost as much boy was roasted as meat.

Ralph dribbled. He meant to refuse meat but his past diet of fruit and nuts, with an odd crab or fish, gave him too little resistance. He accepted a piece of half-raw meat and gnawed it like a wolf.

Piggy spoke, also dribbling.

'Aren't I having none?'

Jack had meant to leave him in doubt, as an assertion of power; but Piggy by advertising his omission made more cruelty necessary.

'You didn't hunt.'

'No more did Ralph,' said Piggy wetly, 'nor Simon.' He amplified. 'There isn't more than a ha'porth of meat in a crab.'

Ralph stirred uneasily. Simon, sitting between the twins and Piggy, wiped his mouth and shoved his piece of meat over the rocks to Piggy, who grabbed it. The twins giggled and Simon lowered his face in shame.

Then Jack leapt to his feet, slashed off a great hunk of meat, and flung it down at Simon's feet.

'Eat! Damn you!'

He glared at Simon.

'Take it!'

He spun on his heel, centre of a bewildered circle of boys.

'I got you meat!'

Numberless and inexpressible frustrations combined to make his rage elemental and awe-inspiring.

'I painted my face – I stole up. Now you eat – all of you – and I –'

Slowly the silence on the mountain-top deepened till the click of the fire and the soft hiss of roasting meat could be heard clearly. Jack looked round for understanding but found only respect. Ralph stood among the ashes of the signal fire, his hands full of meat, saying nothing.

Then at last Maurice broke the silence. He changed the subject to the only one that could bring the majority of them together.

'Where did you find the pig?'

Roger pointed down the unfriendly side.

'They were there – by the sea.'

Jack, recovering, could not bear to have his story told. He broke in quickly.

'We spread round. I crept, on hands and knees. The spears fell out because they hadn't barbs on. The pig ran away and made an awful noise –'

'It turned back and ran into the circle, bleeding –'

All the boys were talking at once, relieved and excited.

'We closed in –'

Pig

The first blow had paralysed its hind quarters, so then the circle could close in and beat and beat –

'I cut the pig's throat –'

The twins, still sharing their identical grin, jumped up and ran round each other. Then the rest joined in, making pig-dying noises and shouting.

'One for his nob!'

'Give him a fourpenny one!'

Then Maurice pretended to be the pig and ran squealing into the centre, and the hunters, circling still, pretended to beat him. As they danced, they sang.

'*Kill the pig. Cut her throat. Bash her in.*'

William Golding: *Lord of the Flies*

PICNICS

Suitors at the picnic

– I remember a sweltering August Sunday. Mother said it would be nice to go out. We would walk a short mile to a nice green spot and boil a kettle under the trees. It sounded simple enough, but we knew better. For mother's picnics were planned on a tribal scale, with huge preparations beforehand. She flew round the kitchen issuing orders and the young men stood appalled at the work. There were sliced cucumbers and pots of paste, radishes, pepper and salt, cakes and buns and macaroons, soup-plates of bread and butter, jam, treacle, jugs of milk, and several fresh-made jellies.

The young men didn't approve of this at all, and muttered it was blooming mad. But with a 'You carry that now, there's a dear boy', each of us carried something. So we set off at last like a frieze of Greeks bearing gifts to some woodland god – Mother, with a tea-cloth over her head, gathering flowers as she went along, the sisters following with cakes and bread, Jack with the kettle, Tony with the salt, myself with a jug of milk; then the scowling youths in their blue serge suits carrying the jellies in open basins – jellies which rapidly melted in the sun and splashed them with yellow and rose. The young men swapped curses under their breath, brother Harold hung back in shame, while Mother led the way with prattling songs determined to make the thing go.

She knew soon enough when people turned sour and moved mountains to charm them out of it, and showed that she knew by a desperate gaiety and by noisy attacks on silence.

'Now come along, Maurice, best foot forward, mind how you go, tee-hee. Leslie! just look at those pretty what-d'you-call'ems – those what's-is – *aren't* they a picture? I said Leslie, look, aren't they pretty, my dear? Funny you don't know the name. Oh, isn't it a scrumptious day, tra-la? Boys, isn't it a scrumptious day?'

Wordy, flustered, but undefeated, she got us to the woods at last. We were ordered to scatter and gather sticks and to build a fire for the kettle. The fire smoked glumly and stung our eyes, the young men sat round like martyrs, the milk turned sour, the butter fried on the bread, cake crumbs got stuck to the cucumber, wasps seized the treacle, the kettle wouldn't boil, and we ended by drinking the jellies.

As we boys would eat anything, anywhere, none of this bothered us much. But the young courting men sat on their spread silk-handkerchiefs and gazed at the meal in horror. 'No thanks, Mrs Lee. I don't think I could. I've just had me dinner, ta.'

They were none of them used to such disorder, didn't care much for open-air picnics – but most of all they were wishing to be away with their girls, away in some field or gully, where summer and love would be food enough, and an absence of us entirely.

Laurie Lee: *Cider with Rosie*

Poet's picnic

There, on a slope of orchard, Francis laid
A damask napkin wrought with horse and hound,
Brought out a dusky loaf that smelt of home,
And, half-cut-down, a pasty costly-made,
Where quail and pigeon, lark and leveret lay,
Like fossils of the rock, with golden yolks
Imbedded and injellied; last, with these,
A flask of cider from his father's vats,
Prime, which I knew; and so we sat and eat
And talked old matters over . . .

Alfred, Lord Tennyson: *Audley Court*

A day on the river

The Mole waggled his toes from sheer happiness, spread his chest with a sigh of full contentment, and leaned back blissfully into the soft cushions. '*What* a day I'm having!' he said. 'Let us start at once!'

'Hold hard a minute, then!' said the Rat. He looped the painter through a ring in his landing-stage, climbed up into his hole above, and after a short interval reappeared staggering under a fat, wicker luncheon-basket.

'Shove that under your feet,' he observed to the Mole, as he passed it down into the boat. Then he untied the painter and took the sculls again.

'What's inside it?' asked the Mole, wriggling with curiosity.

'There's cold chicken inside it,' replied the Rat briefly; 'coldtongue coldhamcoldbeefpickledgherkinssaladfrenchrollscresssandwidges pottedmeatgingerbeerlemonadesodawater —'

'O stop, stop,' cried the Mole in ecstasies: 'This is too much!'

'Do you really think so?' inquired the Rat seriously. 'It's only what I always take on these little excursions; and the other animals are always telling me that I'm a mean beast and cut it *very* fine!'

Kenneth Grahame: *The Wind in the Willows*

Recipe for a salad

To make this condiment your poet begs
The pounded yellow of two hard boiled eggs;
Two boiled potatoes, passed through kitchen sieve,
Smoothness and softness to the salad give.
Let onion atoms lurk within the bowl,
And, half suspected, animate the whole.
Of mordant mustard add a single spoon,
Distrust the condiment that bites so soon;
But deem it not, thou man of herbs, a fault
To add a double quantity of salt;
Four times the spoon with oil of Lucca crown,
And twice with vinegar procured from town;
And lastly o'er the flavour'd compound toss
A magic soupçon of anchovy sauce.
Oh, green and glorious! Oh, herbaceous treat!
'Twould tempt the dying anchorite to eat;
Back to the world he'd turn his fleeting soul,
And plunge his fingers in the salad-bowl!
Serenely full, the epicure would say,
'Fate cannot harm me, I have dined today.'

Sydney Smith

SOUP AND FISH

Chowder

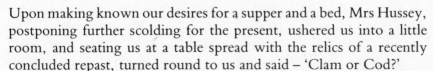

Upon making known our desires for a supper and a bed, Mrs Hussey, postponing further scolding for the present, ushered us into a little room, and seating us at a table spread with the relics of a recently concluded repast, turned round to us and said – 'Clam or Cod?'

'What's that about Cods, ma'am?' said I, with much politeness.

'Clam or Cod?' she repeated.

'A clam for supper? a cold clam; is *that* what you mean, Mrs Hussey?' says I; 'but that's a rather cold and clammy reception in the winter time, ain't it, Mrs Hussey?'

But being in a great hurry to resume scolding the man in the purple shirt, who was waiting for it in the entry, and seeming to hear nothing but the world 'clam', Mrs Hussey hurried towards an open door leading to the kitchen, and bawling out 'clam for two', disappeared.

'Queequeg,' said I, 'do you think that we can make out a supper for us both on one clam?'

However, a warm savory steam from the kitchen served to belie the apparently cheerless prospect before us. But when that smoking chowder came in, the mystery was delightfully explained. Oh, sweet friends! hearken to me. It was made of small juicy clams, scarcely bigger than hazel nuts, mixed with pounded ship biscuit, and salted pork cut up into little flakes; the whole enriched with butter, and plentifully seasoned with pepper and salt. Our appetites being sharpened by the frosty voyage, and in particular, Queequeg seeing his favorite fishing food before him, and the chowder being surpassingly excellent, we despatched it with great expedition: when leaning back a moment and bethinking me of Mrs Hussey's clam and cod announcement, I thought I would try a little experiment. Stepping to the kitchen door, I uttered the word 'cod' with great emphasis, and resumed my seat. In a few moments the savory steam came forth again, but with a different flavor, and in good time a fine cod-chowder was placed before us.

We resumed business; and while plying our spoons in the bowl, thinks I to myself, I wonder now if this here has any effect on the head? What's that stultifying saying about chowder-headed people? 'But look, Queequeg, ain't that a live eel in your bowl? Where's your harpoon?'

Fishiest of all fishy places was the Try Pots, which well deserved its name; for the pots there were always boiling chowders. Chowder for breakfast, and chowder for dinner, and chowder for supper, till you began to look for fish-bones coming through your clothes. The area before the house was paved with clam-shells. Mrs Hussey wore a polished necklace of codfish vertebrae; and Hosea Hussey had his account books bound in superior old shark-skin. There was a fishy flavor to the milk, too, which I could not at all account for, till one morning happening to take a stroll along the beach among some fishermen's boats, I saw Hosea's brindled cow feeding on fish remnants, and marching along the sand with each foot in a cod's decapitated head, looking very slip-shod, I assure ye.

Supper concluded, we received a lamp, and directions from Mrs Hussey concerning the nearest way to bed; but, as Queequeg was about to precede me up the stairs, the lady reached forth her arm, and demanded his harpoon; she allowed no harpoon in her chambers. 'Why not?' said I; 'every true whaleman sleeps with his harpoon – but why not?' 'Because it's dangerous,' says she. 'Ever since young Stiggs coming from that unfort'nt v'y'ge of his, when he was gone four years and a half, with ony three barrels of *ile*, was found dead in my first floor back, with his harpoon in his side; ever since then I allow no boarders to take sich dangerous weepons in their rooms a-night. So, Mr Queequeg' (for she had learned his name), 'I will just take this here iron, and keep it for you till morning. But the chowder; clam or cod tomorrow for breakfast, men?'

'Both,' says I; 'and let's have a couple of smoked herring by way of variety.'

Herman Melville: *Moby Dick*

Salmon for the water bailiff

In times when water bailiffs in Tweed had very small salaries, they themselves were by no means scrupulous about the observance of close time, but partook of the good things of the river in all seasons, lawful or unlawful. There is a man now, I believe, living at Selkirk, who in times of yore used certain little freedoms with the Tweed Act, which did not become the virtue of his office. As a water bailiff he was sworn to tell of all he saw; and indeed, as he said, it could not be expected that he should tell of what he did not see.

When his dinner was served up during close time, his wife usually brought to the table in the first place a platter of potatoes and a napkin; she then bound the latter over his eyes that nothing might offend his sight. This being done, the illegal salmon was brought in smoking hot, and he fell to, blindfolded as he was, like a conscientious water bailiff, – if you know what that is; nor was the napkin taken from his eyes till the fins and bones were removed from the room, and every visible evidence of a salmon having been there had completely vanished: thus he saw no illegal act committed, and went to give in his annual report at Cornhill with his idea of a clear conscience. This was going too near the wind, or rather the water; but what would you have? – the man was literal, and a great eater of Salmon from his youth.

William Scrope: *Days and Nights of Salmon Fishing*

Beautiful soup

'Shall we try another figure of the Lobster Quadrille?' the Gryphon
went on. 'Or would you like the Mock Turtle to sing you a song?'

'Oh, a song, please, if the Mock Turtle would be so kind,' Alice
replied, so eagerly that the Gryphon said in a rather offended tone,
'Hm! No accounting for tastes! Sing her '*Turtle Soup*', will you, old
fellow?'

The Mock Turtle sighed deeply, and began, in a voice sometimes
choked with sobs, to sing this;

> '*Beautiful Soup, so rich and green,*
> *Waiting in a hot tureen!*
> *Who for such dainties would not stoop?*
> *Soup of the evening, beautiful Soup!*
> *Soup of the evening, beautiful Soup!*
> *Beau – ootiful Soo – oop!*
> *Beau – ootiful Soo – oop!*
> *Soo – oop of the e – e – evening,*
> *Beautiful, beautiful Soup!*
>
> *Beautiful Soup! Who cares for fish,*
> *Game, or any other dish?*
> *Who would not give all else for two*
> *pennyworth only of beautiful Soup?*
> *Pennyworth only of beautiful Soup?*
> *Beau – ootiful Soo – oop!*
> *Beau – ootiful Soo – oop!*
> *Soo – oop of the e – e – evening,*
> *Beautiful, beauti – FUL SOUP!'*

'Chorus again!' cried the Gryphon, and the Mock Turtle had just
begun to repeat it, when a cry of 'The trial's beginning!' was heard
in the distance.

'Come on!' cried the Gryphon, and, taking Alice by the hand, it
hurried off, without waiting for the end of the song.

Soup and Fish

'What trial is it?' Alice panted, as she ran; but the Gryphon only answered, 'Come on!' and ran the faster, while more and more faintly came, carried on the breeze that followed them, the melancholy words:

> *Soo – oop of the e – e – evening,*
> *Beautiful, beautiful Soup!*

Lewis Carroll: *Alice's Adventures in Wonderland*

RICH AND STRANGE

Dish of the day

Ford staggered back to the table where Zaphod, Arthur and Trillian were sitting waiting for the fun to begin.

'Gotta have some food,' said Ford.

'Hi, Ford,' said Zaphod, 'you speak to the big noise boy?'

Ford waggled his head noncommitally.

'Hotblack? I sort of spoke to him, yeah.'

'What'd he say?'

'Well, not a lot really. He's . . . er . . .'

'Yeah?'

'He's spending a year dead for tax reasons. I've got to sit down.'

He sat down.

The waiter approached.

'Would you like to see the menu?' he said, 'or would you like to meet the Dish of the Day?'

'Huh?' said Ford.

'Huh?' said Arthur.

'Huh?' said Trillian.

'That's cool,' said Zaphod, 'we'll meet the meat.' . . .

A large dairy animal approached Zaphod Beeblebrox's table, a large fat meaty quadruped of the bovine type with large watery eyes, small horns and what might almost have been an ingratiating smile on its lips.

'Good evening,' it lowed and sat back heavily on its haunches, 'I am the main Dish of the Day. May I interest you in parts of my body?' It harrumphed and gurgled a bit, wriggled its hind quarters into a more comfortable position and gazed peacefully at them.

Its gaze was met by looks of startled bewilderment from Arthur and Trillian, a resigned shrug from Ford Prefect and naked hunger from Zaphod Beeblebrox.

'Something off the shoulder perhaps?' suggested the animal, 'Braised in a white wine sauce?'

'Er, *your* shoulder?' said Arthur in a horrified whisper.

'But naturally my shoulder, sir,' mooed the animal contentedly, 'nobody else's is mine to offer.'

Zaphod leapt to his feet and started prodding and feeling the animal's shoulder appreciatively.

'Or the rump is very good,' murmured the animal. 'I've been exercising it and eating plenty of grain, so there's a lot of good meat there.' It gave a mellow grunt, gurgled again and started to chew the cud. It swallowed the cud again.

'Or a casserole of me perhaps?' it added.

'You mean this animal actually wants us to eat it?' whispered Trillian to Ford.

'Me?' said Ford, with a glazed look in his eyes, 'I don't mean anything.'

'That's absolutely horrible,' exclaimed Arthur, 'the most revolting thing I've ever heard.'

'What's the problem, Earthman?' said Zaphod, now transferring his attention to the animal's enormous rump.

'I just don't want to eat an animal that's standing there inviting me to,' said Arthur, 'it's heartless.'

'Better than eating an animal that doesn't want to be eaten,' said Zaphod.

'That's not the point,' Arthur protested. Then he thought about it for a moment. 'Alright,' he said, 'maybe it is the point. I don't care, I'm not going to think about it now. I'll just . . . er . . .'

The Universe raged about him in its death throes.

'I think I'll just have a green salad,' he muttered.

'May I urge you to consider my liver?' asked the animal, 'it must be very rich and tender by now, I've been force-feeding myself for months.'

'A green salad,' said Arthur emphatically.

'A green salad?' said the animal, rolling his eyes disapprovingly at Arthur.

'Are you going to tell me,' said Arthur, 'that I shouldn't have green salad?'

'Well,' said the animal, 'I know many vegetables that are very clear on that point. Which is why it was eventually decided to cut through the whole tangled problem and breed an animal that actually wanted to be eaten and was capable of saying so clearly and distinctly. And here I am.'

It managed a very slight bow.

'Glass of water please,' said Arthur.

'Look,' said Zaphod, 'we want to eat, we don't want to make a meal of the issues. Four rare steaks please, and hurry. We haven't eaten in five hundred and seventy-six thousand million years.'

The animal staggered to its feet. It gave a mellow gurgle.

'A very wise choice, sir, if I may say so. Very good,' it said, 'I'll just nip off and shoot myself.'

He turned and gave a friendly wink to Arthur.

'Don't worry, sir,' he said, 'I'll be very humane.'

It waddled unhurriedly off to the kitchen.

A matter of minutes later the waiter arrived with four huge steaming steaks. Zaphod and Ford wolfed straight into them without a second's hesitation. Trillian paused, then shrugged and started into hers.

Arthur stared at his feeling slightly ill.

'Hey, Earthman,' said Zaphod with a malicious grin on the face that wasn't stuffing itself, 'what's eating you?'

And the band played on.

Douglas Adams: *The Restaurant at the End of the Universe*

Snake steak supper

When they got to his purple double-wide, Joe Lon skinned snakes in a frenzy. He picked up the snakes by the tails as he dipped them out of the metal drums and swung them around and around his head and then popped them like a cowwhip, which caused their heads to explode. Then he nailed them up on a board in the pen and skinned them out with a pair of wire pliers. Elfie was standing in the door of the trailer behind them with a baby on her hip. Full of beer and fascinated with what Joe Lon was doing, none of them saw her. But Joe Lon could feel – or thought he could – the weight of her gaze on his back while he popped and skinned the snakes. He finally turned and looked at her, pulling his lips back from his teeth in a smile that only shamed him.

He called across the yard to her. 'Thought we'd cook up some snake and stuff, darlin, have ourselves a feast.'

Her face brightened in the door and she said: 'Course we can, Joe Lon, honey.'

Elfie brought him a pan and Joe Lon cut the snakes into half-inch steaks. Duffy turned to Elfie and said: 'My name's Duffy Deeter and this is something fine. Want to tell me how you cook up snakes?'

Elfie smiled, trying not to show her teeth. 'It's lots a ways. Way I do mostly is I soak'm in vinegar about ten minutes, drain'm off good, and sprinkle me a little Looseanner redhot on'm, roll'm in flour, and fry'm is the way I mostly do.'

'God,' said Susan Gender.

Duffy Deeter slapped Joe Lon on the ass and said, 'Where'd you get this little lady, boy? Damn if you haven't got you some little lady here.'

Elfie blushed, and Joe Lon didn't answer. They followed him into the trailer. Joe Lon put on a stack of Merle Haggard and Elfie took the snake into the kitchen, where she wouldn't let the other two girls come, saying: 'It ain't but room for one in a trailer kitchen. I'll cook it up in two shakes.' Joe Lon got some beer out of the icebox and they all sat in the little living room looking out onto the camp-ground. The babies lay in their playpen where their mother had put them, screaming and refusing to suck their sugar-tits. Joe Lon pulled at his beer and then said something to Hard Candy he'd been thinking on and off most of the afternoon.

'Why don't you call you house and tell that sister of yorn to come eat snake with us?' He was unable to make himself say the boy's name. 'Tell'r to bring him that plays debate too if she feels like it. We got enough snake here for everybody.'

Hard Candy got up and called her sister. Directly, she came back and sat down. 'Berenice said she'd be sliding in here in a sec but not to wait the snake on her.'

They all sat now without talking, pulling easy on the beers, a little stunned with alcohol and exhausted with dancing. Susan Gender said she hoped they had not hurt the little Spic and that he'd get back to Mystic all right, but nobody wanted to talk about it, so they let it alone and watched the layering smoke over the campground above the open fires that were starting up now among the trailers and campers and tents. Although it was still about four hours until sundown, the afternoon was beginning to turn cool.

Joe Lon had just come back from the icebox with more beer when Berenice came sliding into the yard beside his pickup in her new Austin-Healy. She had two batons with her, and she came prancing through the door, turning her brilliant smile on all of them, and explaining that Shep had stayed to talk with her daddy because he was seriously considering becoming a brain surgeon.

'Besides,' she said, a little breathless, beaming still, 'the notion of a snake steak supper just made'm want to throw up. Shep's got delicate digestion.'

Harry Crews: *A Feast of Snakes*

Tobacco Tapioca

A keen sudden un-Holly-like enthusiasm for homemaking resulted in several un-Holly-like purchases: at a Parke-Bernet auction she acquired a stag-at-bay hunting tapestry and, from the William Randolph Hearst estate, a gloomy pair of Gothic 'easy' chairs; she bought the complete Modern Library, shelves of classical records, innumerable Metropolitan Museum reproductions (including a statue of a Chinese cat that her own cat hated and hissed at and ultimately broke), a Waring mixer and pressure cooker and a library of cook books. She spent whole hausfrau afternoons slopping about in the sweatbox of her midget kitchen: 'José says I'm better than the Colony. Really, who would have dreamed I had such a great natural talent? A month ago I couldn't scramble eggs.' And still couldn't, for that matter. Simple dishes, steak, a proper salad, were beyond her. Instead, she fed José and occasionally myself *outré* soups (brandied black tarrapin poured into avocado shells), Nero-ish novelties (roasted pheasant stuffed with pomegranates and persimmons), and other dubious innovations (chicken and saffron rice served with a chocolate sauce: 'An East Indian classic, *my* dear.') Wartime sugar and cream rationing restricted her imagination when it came to sweets – nevertheless, she once managed something called Tobacco Tapioca: best not describe it.

Truman Capote: *Breakfast at Tiffany's*

Funeral feast

By these means he won a considerable reputation as an eccentric – a reputation which he crowned by wearing suits of white velvet with gold-laced waistcoats, by sticking a bunch of Parma violets in his shirt-front in lieu of a cravat, and by entertaining men of letters to dinners which were greatly talked about. One of these meals, modelled on an eighteenth-century original, had been a funeral feast to mark the most ludicrous of personal misfortunes. The dining-room, draped in black, opened out on to a garden metamorphosed for the occasion, the paths being strewn with charcoal, the ornamental pond edged with black basalt and filled with ink, and the shrubberies replanted with cypresses and pines. The dinner itself was served on a black cloth adorned with baskets of violets and scabious; candelabra shed an eerie green light over the table and tapers flickered in the chandeliers.

While a hidden orchestra played funeral marches, the guests were waited on by naked negresses wearing only slippers and stockings in cloth of silver embroidered with tears.

Dining off black-bordered plates, the company had enjoyed turtle soup, Russian rye bread, ripe olives from Turkey, caviare, mullet botargo, black puddings from Frankfurt, game served in sauces the colour of liquorice and boot-polish, truffle jellies, chocolate creams, plum-puddings, nectarines, pears in grape-juice syrup, mulberries, and black heart-cherries. From dark-tinted glasses they had drunk the wines of Limagne and Roussillon, of Tenedos, Valdepeñas, and Oporto. And after coffee and walnut cordial, they had rounded off the evening with kvass, porter, and stout.

On the invitations, which were similar to those sent out before more solemn obsequies, this dinner was described as a funeral banquet in memory of the host's virility, lately but only temporarily deceased.

J. K. Huysmans: *Against Nature* (translated by Robert Baldick)

Pearl Vinaigrette

There have been two pearls that were the largest in the whole of history; both were owned by Cleopatra, the last of the Queens of Egypt – they had come down to her through the hands of the Kings of the East. When Antony was gorging daily at recherché banquets, she with a pride at once lofty and insolent, queenly wanton as she was, poured contempt on all his pomp and splendour, and when he asked what additional magnificence could be contrived, replied that she would spend 10,000,000 sesterces on a single banquet. Antony was eager to learn how it could be done, although he thought it was impossible. Consequently bets were made, and on the next day, when the matter was to be decided, she set before Antony a banquet that was indeed splendid, but of the kind served every day – Antony laughing and expostulating at its niggardliness. But she vowed it was a mere additional douceur, and that the banquet would round off the account and her own dinner alone would cost 10,000,000 sesterces, and she ordered the second course to be served. In accordance with previous instructions the servants placed in front of her only a single vessel containing vinegar, the strong rough quality of which can melt pearls. She was at the moment wearing in her ears that remarkable and truly unique work of nature. Antony was full of curiosity to see what in the world she was going to do. She took one earring off and dropped the pearl in the vinegar, and when it was melted swallowed it. Lucius Plancus, who was umpiring the wager, placed his hand on the other pearl when she was preparing to destroy it also in a similar way, and declared that Antony had lost the battle – an ominous remark that came true.

Pliny the Elder: *Natural History*

TIME FOR TEA

Tea with Lydia

We always had tea in a small, bay-windowed, overcrowded room on the south side of the house, adjoining the conservatory. Its walls were papered in patterns of pink and silver roses and its furniture was in a style of ponderous cabriole, touched with ecclesiastical. The legs of chairs and tables, in the shape of claws, grasped everywhere at balls that were like mahogany cannon shot. The upholsterings were mostly of a bright prawn pink unfaded by sun because at the slightest touch of it all blinds and shutters were drawn. The Aspens were not Catholics, but there was a prie-dieu in blue beaded petit-point in one corner; nor were they very musical, but in another corner was a grand piano, a rosewood music stand inlaid with strips of ivory, and a cello in case by the wall. Sometimes if the afternoon was very warm we sat at open french windows, through which all the scents of the park and the gardens came to us in exquisite waves, rose with azalea, pink with hawthorn, some wonderfully indeterminate breath of high summer and strawberry with a drowsy flavour of hay.

There were rarely, I think, more than the five of us there: the two Aspen sisters, Rollo and Lydia and myself; and it suited my vanity to be so very privileged. A maid with her appropriate dragon-flies of starched apron strings brought tea at four o'clock and Rollo lit the burner under a small silver methylated spirit kettle. Either Miss Juliana or Miss Bertie poured tea, one on one Sunday, one on another. 'It's Juley's Sunday,' they would say, or 'it's Bertie's Sunday.' Rollo and I handed round plates of thinnest triangular bread and butter in three varieties of white and brown and a pleasant sugar-browned loaf of currant bread. Sometimes Rollo called me 'Old fellow' or made a remark about pheasants or spoke of how plum awful something was. Miss Juliana, in her assertive jolly way, rattled on about this and that until arrested with firmness by Miss Bertie on some point of dry, irrefutable fact about the nature or history of the town. Most of the time Lydia and I sat looking at each other.

There was an amazing, beautiful frenzy about these quiet tea-times. There was a sort of suspended inner fieriness about us both that was painful and lovely. Sometimes we could not bear any longer to look at each other and I felt myself caught up again in a sort of entangling web, enraptured and baffled. She always wore dresses of silk on Sunday and their smooth peel-like softness, growing tighter all the summer as her body filled out, was drawn over her breasts with startling clearness whenever she moved.

H. E. Bates: *Love for Lydia*

The Mad Hatter's tea party

Alice looked all round the table, but there was nothing on it but tea. 'I don't see any wine,' she remarked.

'There isn't any,' said the March Hare.

'Then it wasn't very civil of you to offer it,' said Alice angrily.

'It wasn't very civil of you to sit down without being invited,' said the March Hare.

'I didn't know it was *your* table,' said Alice; 'it's laid for a great many more than three.'

'Your hair wants cutting,' said the Hatter. He had been looking at Alice for some time with great curiosity, and this was his first speech.

'You should learn not to make personal remarks,' Alice said with some severity; 'it's very rude.'

The Hatter opened his eyes very wide on hearing this; but all he *said* was 'Why is a raven like a writing-desk?'

'Come, we shall have some fun now!' thought Alice. 'I'm glad they've begun asking riddles. – I believe I can guess that,' she added aloud.

'Do you mean that you think you can find out the answer to it?' said the March Hare.

'Exactly so,' said Alice.

'Then you should say what you mean,' the March Hare went on.

'I do,' Alice hastily replied; 'at least – at least I mean what I say – that's the same thing, you know.'

'Not the same thing a bit!' said the Hatter. 'Why, you might just as well say that "I see what I eat" is the same thing as "I eat what I see"!'

'You might just as well say,' added the March Hare, 'that "I like what I get" is the same thing as "I get what I like"!'

'You might just as well say,' added the Dormouse, which seemed to be talking in his sleep, 'that "I breathe when I sleep" is the same thing as "I sleep when I breathe"!'

'It *is* the same thing with you,' said the Hatter; and here the conversation dropped . . .

Lewis Carroll: *Alice's Adventures in Wonderland*

Gwendolen versus Cecily

Enter MERRIMAN, *followed by the footman. He carries a salver, table cloth, and plate stand.* CECILY *is about to retort. The presence of the servants exercises a restraining influence, under which both girls chafe*

MERRIMAN   Shall I lay tea here as usual, Miss?

CECILY [*sternly, in a calm voice*]   Yes, as usual.

   [MERRIMAN *begins to clear table and lay cloth. A long pause.* CECILY *and* GWENDOLEN *glare at each other*

GWENDOLEN   Are there many interesting walks in the vicinity, Miss Cardew?

CECILY   Oh yes! a great many. From the top of one of the hills quite close one can see five counties.

GWENDOLEN   Five counties! I don't think I should like that; I hate crowds.

CECILY [*sweetly*]   I suppose that is why you live in town?

[GWENDOLEN *bites her lip, and beats her foot nervously with her parasol*

GWENDOLEN [*looking round*]   Quite a well-kept garden this is, Miss Cardew.

CECILY   So glad you like it, Miss Fairfax.

GWENDOLEN   I had no idea there were any flowers in the country.

CECILY   Oh, flowers are as common here, Miss Fairfax, as people are in London.

GWENDOLEN   Personally I cannot understand how anybody manages to exist in the country, if anybody who is anybody does. The country always bores me to death.

CECILY   Ah! This is what the newspapers call agricultural depression, is it not? I believe the aristocracy are suffering very much from it just at present. It is almost an epidemic amongst them, I have been told. May I offer you some tea, Miss Fairfax?

GWENDOLEN [*with elaborate politeness*]   Thank you. [*Aside.*] Detestable girl! But I require tea!

CECILY [*sweetly*]   Sugar?

GWENDOLEN [*superciliously*]   No, thank you. Sugar is not fashionable any more.

[CECILY *looks angrily at her, takes up the tongs and puts four lumps of sugar into the cup*

CECILY [*severely*]   Cake or bread and butter?

GWENDOLEN [*in a bored manner*]   Bread and butter, please. Cake is rarely seen at the best houses nowadays.

CECILY [*cuts a very large slice of cake and puts it on the tray*]   Hand that to Miss Fairfax.

[MERRIMAN *does so, and goes out with footman.*

GWENDOLEN *drinks the tea and makes a grimace. Puts down cup at once, reaches out her hand to the bread and butter, looks at it, and finds it is cake. Rises in indignation*

GWENDOLEN   You have filled my tea with lumps of sugar, and though I asked most distinctly for bread and butter, you have given me cake. I am known for the gentleness of my disposition, and the extraordinary sweetness of my nature, but I warn you, Miss Cardew, you may go too far.

CECILY [*rising*]   To save my poor, innocent, trusting boy from the machinations of any other girl there are no lengths to which I would not go.

GWENDOLEN   From the moment I saw you I distrusted you. I felt that you were false and deceitful. I am never deceived in such matters. My first impressions of people are invariably right.

CECILY   It seems to me, Miss Fairfax, that I am trespassing on your valuable time. No doubt you have many other calls of a similar character to make in the neighbourhood.

Oscar Wilde: *The Importance of Being Earnest*

High tea at Micmash

It may have been a splendid gathering but it was certainly a very odd meal. Inigo remembered other high teas but none higher than this. The forms were a solid mass of eaters and drinkers and the tables were a solid mass of food. There were hams and tongues and rounds of cold beef and raised pies and egg salads; plates heaped high with white bread, brown bread, currant tea cakes, scones; dishes of jelly and custard and blancmange and fruit salad; piles of jam tarts and maids-of-honour and cream puffs and almond tarts; then walnut cake, plumcake, chocolate cake, coconut cake; mounds of sugar, quarts of cream and a steady flood of tea. Inigo never remembered seeing quite so much food before. It was like being asked to eat one's way through the Provision and Cooked Food departments of one of the big stores. The appetite was not tickled, not even met fairly; it was overwhelmed. The sight of these tables drove hunger out of the world, made it impossible to imagine it had ever been there. Inigo ate this and that, but he hardly knew what he was eating, he was so warm, so tightly wedged in, so amazed at the spectacle. The Second Resurrectionists were worthy of the colossal meal spread before them. This highest of high teas had met its match. If they had all been forty years in the wilderness they could not have dealt with it more manfully. They were not your gabbling, laughing eaters; they did not make a first rush and then suddenly lose heart; they did not try this and taste that. No, they were quiet, systematic, devastating;

175

they advanced steadily, in good order from the first slice of ham to the last slice of chocolate cake; and in fifty minutes the tables were a mere ruin of broken meats, the flood of tea a pale and tepid trickle.

J. B. Priestley: *The Good Companions*

FOOTING THE BILL

The East Acton Volunteer Ball

APRIL 16. The night of the East Acton Volunteer Ball. On my advice, Carrie put on the same dress that she looked so beautiful in at the Mansion House, for it had occurred to me, being a military ball, that Mr Perkupp, who, I believe, is an officer in the Honourable Artillery Company, would in all probability be present. Lupin, in his usual incomprehensible language, remarked that he had heard it was a 'bounders' ball'. I didn't ask him what he meant though I didn't understand. Where he gets these expressions from I don't know; he certainly doesn't learn them at home.

The invitation was for half-past eight, so I concluded if we arrived an hour later we should be in good time, without being 'unfashionable', as Mrs James says. It was very difficult to find – the cabman having to get down several times to inquire at different public-houses where the Drill Hall was. I wonder at people living in such out-of-the-way places. No one seemed to know it. However, after going up and down a good many badly-lighted streets we arrived at our destination. I had no idea it was so far away from Holloway. I gave the cabman five shillings, who only grumbled, saying it was dirt cheap at half-a-sovereign, and was impertinent enough to advise me the next time I went to a ball to take a 'bus.

Captain Welcut received us, saying we were rather late, but that it was better late than never. He seemed a very good-looking gentleman though, as Carrie remarked, 'rather short for an officer'. He begged to be excused for leaving us, as he was engaged for a dance, and hoped we should make ourselves at home. Carrie took my arm and we walked round the rooms two or three times and watched the people dancing. I couldn't find a single person I knew, but attributed it to most of them being in uniform. As we were entering the supper-room I received a slap on the shoulder, followed by a welcome shake of the hand. I said: 'Mr Padge, I believe?' He replied: 'That's right.'

I gave Carrie a chair, and seated by her was a lady who made herself at home with Carrie at once.

There was a very liberal repast on the tables, plenty of champagne, claret, etc., and, in fact, everything seemed to be done regardless of expense. Mr Padge is a man that, I admit, I have no particular liking for, but I felt so glad to come across someone I knew, that I asked him to sit at our table, and I must say that for a short fat man he looked well in uniform, although I think his tunic was rather baggy in the back. It was the only supper-room that I have been in that was not over-crowded; in fact we were the only people there, everybody being so busy dancing.

I assisted Carrie and her newly-formed acquaintance, who said her name was Lupkin, to some champagne; also myself, and handed the bottle to Mr Padge to do likewise, saying: 'You must look after yourself.' He replied: 'That's right,' and poured out half a tumbler and drank Carrie's health, coupled, as he said, 'with her worthy lord and master'. We all had some splendid pigeon pie, and ices to follow.

The waiters were very attentive, and asked if we would like some more wine. I assisted Carrie and her friend and Mr Padge, also some people who had just come from the dancing-room, who were very civil. It occurred to me at the time that perhaps some of the gentlemen knew me in the City, as they were so polite. I made myself useful, and assisted several ladies to ices, remembering an old saying that 'There is nothing lost by civility'.

The band struck up for the dance, and they all went into the ball-room. The ladies (Carrie and Mrs Lupkin) were anxious to see the dancing, and as I had not quite finished my supper, Mr Padge offered his arms to them and escorted them to the ball-room, telling me to follow. I said to Mr Padge: 'It is quite a West End affair,' to which remark Mr Padge replied: 'That's right.'

When I had quite finished my supper, and was leaving, the waiter who had been attending on us arrested my attention by tapping me on the shoulder. I thought it unusual for a waiter at a private ball to expect a tip, but nevertheless gave a shilling, as he had been very attentive. He smilingly replied: 'I beg your pardon, sir, this is no good,' alluding to the shilling. 'Your party's had four suppers at 5s. a head, five ices at 1s., three bottles of champagne at 11s. 6d., a glass of claret, and a sixpenny cigar for the stout gentleman – in all £3 0s. 6d.!'

I don't think I was ever so surprised in my life, and had only sufficient breath to inform him that I had received a private invitation, to which he answered that he was perfectly well aware of that; but that the invitation didn't include eatables and drinkables. A gentleman who was standing at the bar corroborated the waiter's statement, and assured me it was quite correct.

The waiter said he was extremely sorry if I had been under any misapprehension; but it was not his fault. Of course there was nothing to be done but to pay. So, after turning out my pockets, I just managed to scrape up sufficient, all but nine shillings; but the manager, on my giving my card to him, said: 'That's all right.'

I don't think I ever felt more humiliated in my life . . .

George and Weedon Grossmith: *The Diary of a Nobody*

Just one thing for luncheon

I caught sight of her at the play and in answer to her beckoning I went over during the interval and sat down beside her. It was long since I had last seen her and if someone had not mentioned her name I hardly think I would have recognised her. She addressed me brightly.

'Well, it's many years since we first met. How time does fly! We're none of us getting any younger. Do you remember the first time I saw you? You asked me to luncheon.'

Did I remember?

It was twenty years ago and I was living in Paris. I had a tiny apartment in the Latin Quarter overlooking a cemetery and I was earning barely enough money to keep body and soul together. She had read a book of mine and had written to me about it. I answered, thanking her, and presently I received from her another letter saying that she was passing through Paris and would like to have a chat with me; but her time was limited and the only free moment she had was on the following Thursday; she was spending the morning at the

Luxembourg and would I give her a little luncheon at Foyot's afterwards? Foyot's is a restaurant at which the French senators eat and it was so far beyond my means that I had never even thought of going there. But I was flattered and I was too young to have learned to say no to a woman. (Few men, I may add, learn this until they are too old to make it of any consequence to a woman what they say.) I had eighty francs (gold francs) to last me the rest of the month and a modest luncheon should not cost more than fifteen. If I cut out coffee for the next two weeks I could manage well enough.

I answered that I would meet my friend – by correspondence – at Foyot's on Thursday at half-past twelve. She was not so young as I expected and in appearance imposing rather than attractive. She was in fact a woman of forty (a charming age, but not one that excites a sudden and devastating passion at first sight), and she gave me the impression of having more teeth, white and large and even, than were necessary for any practical purpose. She was talkative, but since she seemed inclined to talk about me I was prepared to be an attentive listener.

I was startled when the bill of fare was brought, for the prices were a great deal higher than I had anticipated. But she reassured me.

'I never eat anything for luncheon,' she said.

'Oh, don't say that!' I answered generously.

'I never eat more than one thing. I think people eat far too much nowadays. A little fish, perhaps. I wonder if they have any salmon.'

Well, it was early in the year for salmon and it was not on the bill of fare, but I asked the waiter if there was any. Yes, a beautiful salmon had just come in, it was the first they had had. I ordered it for my guest. The waiter asked her if she would have something while it was being cooked.

'No,' she answered, 'I never eat more than one thing. Unless you had a little caviare. I never mind caviare.'

My heart sank a little. I knew I could not afford caviare, but I could not very well tell her that. I told the waiter by all means to bring caviare. For myself I chose the cheapest dish on the menu and that was a mutton chop.

'I think you're unwise to eat meat,' she said. 'I don't know how you can expect to work after eating heavy things like chops. I don't believe in overloading my stomach.'

Then came the question of drink.

'I never drink anything for luncheon,' she said.

'Neither do I,' I answered promptly.

'Except white wine,' she proceeded as though I had not spoken. 'These French white wines are so light. They're wonderful for the digestion.'

'What would you like?' I asked, hospitable still, but not exactly effusive.

She gave me a bright and amicable flash of her white teeth.

'My doctor won't let me drink anything but champagne.'

I fancy I turned a trifle pale. I ordered half a bottle. I mentioned casually that my doctor had absolutely forbidden me to drink champagne.

'What are you going to drink, then?'

'Water.'

She ate the caviare and she ate the salmon. She talked gaily of art and literature and music. But I wondered what the bill would come to. When my mutton chop arrived she took me quite seriously to task.

'I see that you're in the habit of eating a heavy luncheon. I'm sure it's a mistake. Why don't you follow my example and just eat one thing? I'm sure you'd feel ever so much better for it.'

'I *am* only going to eat one thing,' I said, as the waiter came again with the bill of fare.

She waved him aside with an airy gesture.

'No, no, I never eat anything for luncheon. Just a bite, I never want more than that, and I eat that more as an excuse for conversation than anything else. I couldn't possible eat anything more – unless they had some of those giant asparagus. I should be sorry to leave Paris without having some of them.'

My heart sank. I had seen them in the shops and I knew that they were horribly expensive. My mouth had often watered at the sight of them.

'Madame wants to know if you have any of those giant asparagus,' I asked the waiter.

I tried with all my might to will him to say no. A happy smile spread over his broad, priest-like face, and he assured me that they had some so large, so splendid, so tender, that it was a marvel.

'I'm not in the least hungry,' my guest sighed, 'but if you insist I don't mind having some asparagus.'

I ordered them.

'Aren't you going to have any?'

'No, I never eat asparagus.'

'I know there are people who don't like them. The fact is, you ruin your palate by all the meat you eat.'

We waited for the asparagus to be cooked. Panic seized me. It was not a question now how much money I should have left over for the rest of the month, but whether I had enough to pay the bill. It would be mortifying to find myself ten francs short and be obliged to borrow from my guest. I could not bring myself to do that. I knew exactly how much I had and if the bill came to more I made up my mind that I would put my hand in my pocket and with a dramatic cry start up and say it had been picked. Of course it would be awkward if she had not money enough either to pay the bill. Then the only thing would be to leave my watch and say I would come back and pay later.

The asparagus appeared. They were enormous, succulent and appetising. The smell of the melted butter tickled my nostrils as the nostrils of Jehovah were tickled by the burned offerings of the virtuous Semites. I watched the abandoned woman thrust them down her throat in large voluptuous mouthfuls and in my polite way I discoursed on the condition of the drama in the Balkans. At last she finished.

'Coffee?' I said.

'Yes, just an ice-cream and coffee,' she answered.

I was past caring now, so I ordered coffee for myself and an ice-cream and coffee for her.

'You know, there's one thing I thoroughly believe in,' she said, as she ate the ice-cream. 'One should always get up from a meal feeling one could eat a little more.'

'Are you still hungry?' I asked faintly.

'Oh, no, I'm not hungry; you see, I don't eat luncheon. I have a cup of coffee in the morning and then dinner, but I never eat more than one thing for luncheon. I was speaking for you.'

'Oh, I see!'

Then a terrible thing happened. While we were waiting for the coffee, the head waiter, with an ingratiating smile on his false face, came up to us bearing a large basket full of huge peaches. They had the blush of an innocent girl; they had the rich tone of an Italian landscape. But surely peaches were not in season then? Lord knew what they cost. I knew too – a little later, for my guest, going on with her conversation, absentmindedly took one.

'You see, you've filled your stomach with a lot of meat' – my one miserable little chop – 'and you can't eat any more. But I've just had a snack and I shall enjoy a peach.'

The bill came and when I paid it I found that I had only enough for a quite inadequate tip. Her eyes rested for an instant on the three francs I left for the waiter and I knew that she thought me mean. But when I walked out of the restaurant I had the whole month before me and not a penny in my pocket.

'Follow my example,' she said as we shook hands, 'and never eat more than one thing for luncheon.'

'I'll do better than that,' I retorted. 'I'll eat nothing for dinner to-night.'

'Humorist!' she cried gaily, jumping into a cab. 'You're quite a humorist!'

But I have had my revenge at last. I do not believe that I am a vindictive man, but when the immortal gods take a hand in the matter it is pardonable to observe the result with complacency. To-day she weighs twenty-one stone.

W. Somerset Maugham: *The Luncheon*

FOREIGN FOOD

A ferocious curry

Last week a man [called] Mulk Raj Anand made a big curry for everyone about. The first course was beans, little ones. I ate two and couldn't speak. A little man called Wallace B. Nichols, who has made a small fortune out of epic poems on people like Cromwell and Nelson and Mrs Elsie Guddy, took a whole mouthful and was assisted out. He writes for The Cornhill. After the main dish, which was so unbelievably hot that everyone, except the Indian, was crying like Shirley Temple, a woman, Mrs Henderson, looked down on to her plate and saw, lying at one corner of it, a curious rubbery thing that looked like a red, discarded French letter. In interest, she picked it up and found it was the entire skin from her tongue.

(Letter from Dylan Thomas to Pamela Hansford Johnson, 6 August 1937)

Dylan Thomas: *Collected Letters* (edited by Paul Ferris)

Nasty, greasy stuff

Very hungry, accustomed to English post-war food, Grace thought the meal which followed the most delicious she had ever eaten. The food, the wine, the heat and the babel of French talk, most of which was quite incomprehensible to her untuned ear, induced a half-drunk, entirely happy state of haziness. When, after nearly two hours, the party rose from the table, she was floating on air. Everybody wandered off in different directions, and Charles-Edouard announced that he was going to be shut up in the library for the afternoon with his tenants and the agent.

'Will you be happy?' he said, stroking Grace's hair and laughing at her for being, as he could see, so tipsy.

'Oh I'm sleepy and happy and hot and sleepy and drunk and happy and sleepy. It's too blissful being so drunk and happy.'

'Then go to sleep, and when I've finished we'll do whatever you like. Motor down to the sea if you like, and bathe. I'm sleepy myself, but the *régisseur* has convened all these people to see me – they've been waiting too long already – I must go to them, so there it is. See you presently.'

'All right. I'll go and have a little word with Nanny and then a lovely hot sleep. Oh the weather! Oh the bliss of everything! Oh how happy I am!'

Charles-Edouard gave her a very loving look as he went off. He thought he was going to like her even more in France than in England, and was well satisfied to have come back accompanied by this happy beauty.

Alas for the hot, tipsy sleep! Nanny sobered and woke her up all right, her expression alone was a wave of icy water. Grace did not even bother to say 'Wasn't the luncheon delicious? Did you enjoy it?' She just stood and meekly waited for the wave to break over her head.

'Well, dear, we've had nothing to eat since you saw us, nothing whatever. Course upon course of nasty greasy stuff smelling of garlic – a month's ration of meat, yes, but quite raw you know – shame, really – I wasn't going to touch it, let alone give it to Sigi, poor little mite.'

'Nanny says the cheese was matured in manure,' Sigi chipped in, eyes like saucers.

'I wish you could have smelt it, dear, awful it was, and still covered with bits of straw. Makes you wonder, doesn't it? Well, we just had a bite of bread and butter and a few of Mrs Crispin's nice rock cakes I happened to have with me. Not much of a dinner, was it? Funny-looking bread here, too, all crust and holes, I don't know how you'd make a nice bit of damp toast with that. Poor little hungry boy – never mind, it's all right now, darling, your mummy will go to the kitchen for us and ask for some cold ham or chicken – a bit of something plain – some tomatoes, without that nasty, oily, oniony dressing, and a nice floury potato, won't you, dear?'

These words were uttered in tones of command. An order had been issued, there was nothing of the request about them.

'Goodness, I've no idea what floury potato is in French,' said Grace, playing for time. 'Didn't you like the food, Sigi?'

'It's not a question of like it or not like it. The child will eat anything, as you know, but I'm not going to risk having him laid up with a liver attack. This heat wave is quite trying enough without that, thank you very much, not to mention typhoid fever, or worse, I only wish you could have smelt the cheese, that's all I say.'

'I did smell it, we had it downstairs – delicious.'

'Well it may be all right for grown-up people, if that's the sort of thing they go in for,' said Nanny, with a tremendous sniff, 'but give it to the child I will not, and personally I'd rather go hungry.'

Nancy Mitford: *The Blessing*

A hostel lunch

Thatcher reappeared to take their orders.

'Chicken omelette,' Halfacre said. 'Grilled plaice, side salad, no dressing. Sancerre OK for you, Henderson?'

'Lovely.' Henderson' eyes skittered desperately over the menu searching first for something he liked, then for something he recognised. Halfacre's requests didn't even seem to be listed here. This sort of man ordered what he wanted, not what was offered.

'I'll, um, start with the, ah, *crevettes fumées aux framboises*. Followed by . . .' Jesus Christ. 'Followed by . . . Filet Mignon with butterscotch sauce.'

'Vegetables, sir?'

Henderson looked. Salsify, fenugreek, root ginger. What were these things? He saw one that was familiar. 'Braised radishes.'

The menus were removed.

'Sorry, Pruitt,' he said, flapping out his napkin. 'There was something you wanted to talk to me about.'

Pruitt was drawing furrows on the thick white linen of the table-cloth with the tines of his fork.

'That's right.' He paused. 'How would you react, Henderson, if I said . . . If I said that the one word I associate with you is "hostel"?'

'"Hostel?"' His mind raced. 'As in "Youth Hostel"?'

'No, for God's sake. As in hostel aircraft, hostel country, as in "The Soviets are hostel to American policy."'

'Oh. Got you. We stay "style". "Hostyle."'

'Why,' Pruitt now held his fork with both hands as if he might bend it, 'why do you hate me, Henderson? Why do I sense this incredible aggression coming from you?'

William Boyd: *Stars and Bars*

Germans at meat

Bread soup was placed upon the table. 'Ah,' said the Herr Rat, leaning upon the table as he peered into the tureen, 'that is what I need. My *Magen* has not been in order for several days. Bread soup, and just the right consistency. I am a good cook myself' – he turned to me.

'How interesting,' I said, attempting to infuse just the right amount of enthusiasm into my voice.

'Oh yes – when one is not married it is necessary. As for me, I have had all I wanted from women without marriage.' He tucked his napkin into his collar and blew upon his soup as he spoke. 'Now at nine o'clock I make myself an English breakfast, but not much. Four slices of bread, two eggs, two slices of cold ham, one plate of soup, two cups of tea – that is nothing to you.'

He asserted the fact so vehemently that I had not the courage to refute it.

All eyes were suddenly turned upon me. I felt I was bearing the burden of the nation's preposterous breakfast – I who drank a cup of coffee while buttoning my blouse in the morning.

'Nothing at all,' cried Herr Hoffmann from Berlin. '*Ach*, when I was in England in the morning I used to eat.'

He turned up his eyes and his moustache, wiping the soup drippings from his coat and waistcoat.

'Do they really eat so much?' asked Fräulein Stiegelauer. 'Soup and baker's bread and pig's flesh, and tea and coffee and stewed fruit, and honey and eggs, and cold fish and kidneys, and hot fish and liver? All the ladies eat too, especially the ladies.'

'Certainly. I myself have noticed it, when I was living in a hotel in Leicester Square,' cried the Herr Rat. 'It was a good hotel, but they could not make tea – now –'

'Ah, that's one thing I *can* do,' said I, laughing brightly. 'I can make very good tea. The great secret is to warm the teapot.'

'Warm the teapot,' interrupted the Herr Rat, pushing away his soup plate. 'What do you warm the teapot for? Ha! ha! that's very good! One does not eat the teapot, I suppose?'

He fixed his cold blue eyes upon me with an expression which suggested a thousand premeditated invasions.

'So that is the great secret of your English tea? All you do is to warm the teapot.'

I wanted to say that was only the preliminary canter, but could not translate it, and so was silent.

The servant brought in veal, with sauerkraut and potatoes.

'I eat sauerkraut with great pleasure,' said the Traveller from North Germany, 'but now I have eaten so much of it that I cannot retain it. I am immediately forced to –'

'A beautiful day,' I cried, turning to Fräulein Stiegelauer. 'Did you get up early?'

'At five o'clock I walked for ten minutes in the wet grass. Again in bed. At half past five I fell asleep and woke at seven, when I made an "overbody" washing! Again in bed. At eight o'clock I had a cold-water poultice, and at half past eight I drank a cup of mint tea. At nine I drank some malt coffee, and began my "cure". Pass me the sauerkraut, please. You do not eat it?'

'No, thank you. I still find it a little strong.'

'Is it true,' asked the Widow, picking her teeth with a hairpin as she spoke, 'that you are a vegetarian?'

'Why, yes; I have not eaten meat for three years.'

'Im-possible! Have you any family?'

'No.'

'There now, you see, that's what you're coming to! Who ever

heard of having children upon vegetables? It is not possible. But you never have large families in England now; I suppose you are too busy with your suffragetting. Now I have had nine children, and they are all alive, thank God. Fine, healthy babies – though after the first one was born I had to –'

'How *wonderful!*' I cried.

'Wonderful,' said the Widow contemptuously, replacing the hair-pin in the knob which was balanced on the top of her head. 'Not at all! A friend of mine had four at the same time. Her husband was so pleased he gave a supper-party and had them placed on the table. Of course she was very proud.'

'Germany,' boomed the Traveller, biting round a potato which he had speared with his knife, 'is the home of the Family.'

Followed an appreciative silence.

The dishes were changed for beef, red currants and spinach. They wiped their forks upon black bread and started again.

'How long are you remaining here?' asked the Herr Rat.

'I do not know exactly. I must be back in London in September.'

'Of course you will visit München?'

'I am afraid I shall not have time. You see, it is important not to break into my "cure".'

'But you *must* go to München. You have not seen Germany if you have not been to München. All the Exhibitions, all the Art and Soul life of Germany are in München. There is the Wagner Festival in August, and Mozart and a Japanese collection of pictures – and there is the beer! You do not know what good beer is until you have been to Müchen. Why, I see fine ladies every afternoon, but fine ladies, I tell you, drinking glasses so high.' He measured a good wash-stand pitcher in height, and I smiled.

'If I drink a great deal of München beer I sweat so,' said Herr Hoffmann. 'When I am here, in the fields or before my baths, I sweat, but I enjoy it; but in the town it is not at all the same thing.'

Prompted by the thought, he wiped his neck and face with his dinner napkin and carefully cleaned his ears.

A glass dish of stewed apricots was placed upon the table.

'Ah, fruit!' said Fräulein Stiegelauer, 'that is so necessary to health. The doctor told me this morning that the more fruit I could eat the better.'

She very obviously followed the advice.

Said the Traveller: 'I suppose you are frightened of an invasion too, eh? Oh, that's good. I've been reading all about your English play in a newspaper. Did you see it?'

'Yes.' I sat upright. 'I assure you we are not afraid.'

'Well, then, you ought to be,' said the Herr Rat. 'You have got no army at all – a few little boys with their veins full of nicotine poisoning.'

'Don't be afraid,' Herr Hoffmann said. 'We don't want England. If we did we would have had her long ago. We really do not want you.'

He waved his spoon airily, looking across at me as though I were a little child whom he would keep or dismiss as he pleased.

'We certainly do not want Germany,' I said.

'This morning I took a half bath. Then this afternoon I must take a knee bath and an arm bath,' volunteered the Herr Rat; 'then I do my exercises for an hour, and my work is over. A glass of wine and a couple of rolls with some sardines –'

They were handed cherry cake with whipped cream.

'What is your husband's favourite meat?' asked the Widow.

'I really do not know,' I answered.

'You really do not know? How long have you been married?'

'Three years.'

'But you cannot be in earnest! You would not have kept house as his wife for a week without knowing that fact.'

'I really never asked him; he is not at all particular about his food.'

A pause. They all looked at me, shaking their heads, their mouths full of cherry stones.

'No wonder there is a repetition in England of that dreadful state of things in Paris,' said the Widow, folding her dinner napkin. 'How can a woman expect to keep her husband if she does not know his favourite food after three years?'

'*Mahlzeit!*'

'*Mahlzeit!*'

I closed the door after me.

Katherine Mansfield: *In a German Pension*

Lunch with the bishop

'But the steak . . .' Teresa said.

'What about the steak?'

'You can't give the bishop horsemeat.'

'My steak is horsemeat?'

'It always has been. How can I give you beef with the money you allow me?'

'You have nothing else?'

'Nothing.'

'Oh dear, oh dear. We can only pray that he doesn't notice. After all, I have never noticed.'

'*You* have never eaten anything better.'

Father Quixote returned to the bishop in a troubled state of mind, carrying with him a half-bottle of malaga. He was glad when the bishop accepted a glass and then a second one. Perhaps the drink might confuse his tastebuds. He had settled himself deeply in Father Quixote's only easy chair. Father Quixote watched him with anxiety. The bishop didn't look dangerous. He had a very smooth face which might never have known a razor. Father Quixote regretted that he had neglected to shave that morning after early Mass which he had celebrated in an empty church.

'You're on holiday, monsignor?'

'Not exactly on holiday, though it is true I am enjoying my change from Rome. The Holy Father has entrusted me with a little confidential mission because of my knowledge of Spanish. I suppose, father, that you see a great many foreign tourists in El Toboso.'

'Not many, monsignor, for there is very little for them to see here, except for the Museum.'

'What do you keep in the Museum?'

'It is a very small museum, monsignor, one room. No bigger than my parlour. It holds nothing of interest except the signatures.'

'What do you mean by the signatures? May I perhaps have another glass of malaga? Sitting in the sun in that broken-down car has made me very thirsty.'

'Forgive me, monsignor. You see how unused I am to being a host.'

'I have never encountered before a Museum of Signatures.'

'You see, a Mayor of El Toboso years ago began writing to heads of state asking for translations of Cervantes with a signature. The collection is quite remarkable. Of course there is General Franco's signature in what I would call the master copy, and there is Mussolini's and Hitler's (very tiny, his, like a fly's mess) and Churchill's and Hindenburg's and someone called Ramsay MacDonald – I suppose he was the Prime Minister of Scotland.'

'Of England, father.'

Teresa came in with the steaks and they seated themselves at table and the bishop said grace.

Father Quixote poured out the wine and watched with apprehension as the bishop took his first slice of steak, which he quickly washed down with wine – perhaps to take away the taste.

'It is a very common wine, monsignor, but here we are very proud of what we call the manchegan.'

'The wine is agreeable,' the bishop said, 'but the steak . . . the steak,' he said, staring at his plate while Father Quixote waited for the worst, 'the steak . . .' he said a third time as though he were seeking deep in his memory of ancient rites for the correct term of anathema – Teresa meanwhile hovered in the doorway, waiting too – 'never, at any table, have I tasted . . . so tender, so flavoursome, I am tempted to be blasphemous and say so divine a steak. I would like to congratulate your admirable housekeeper.'

'She is here, monsignor.'

'My dear lady, let me shake your hand.' The bishop held out his beringed palm down as though he expected a kiss rather than a shake. Teresa backed hurriedly into the kitchen. 'Did I say something wrong?' the bishop asked.

'No, no, monsignor. It is only that she is unaccustomed to cooking for a bishop.'

'She has a plain and honest face. In these days one *is* often embarrassed to find even in Italy very *marriageable* housekeepers – and alas! only too often marriage does follow.'

Teresa came rapidly in with some cheese and retired at the same speed.

'A little of our *queso manchego*, monsignor?'

'And perhaps another glass of wine to go with it?'

Father Quixote began to feel warm and comfortable. He was encouraged to press a question which he wouldn't have dared to ask his own bishop. A Roman bishop after all was closer to the fount of faith, and the bishop's welcome to the steak of horsemeat encouraged him. It was not for nothing that he had called his Seat 600 Rocinante, and he was more likely to receive a favourable answer if he spoke of her as a horse.

'Monsignor,' he said, 'there is one question I have often asked myself, a question which is perhaps likely to occur more frequently to a countryman than to a city dweller.' He hesitated like a swimmer on a cold brink. 'Would you consider it heretical to pray to God for the life of a horse?'

Graham Greene: *Monsignor Quixote*

The crocodile

Whatever our faults, we can always engage
That no fancy or fable shall sully our page,
   So take note of what follows, I beg.
This creature so grand and august in its age,
   In its youth is hatched out of an egg.
And oft in some far Coptic town
The Missionary sits him down
   To breakfast by the Nile:
The heart beneath his priestly gown
   Is innocent of guile;
When suddenly the rigid frown
Of Panic is observed to drown
   His customary smile.

Foreign Food

Why does he start and leap amain,
And scour the sandy Libyan plain
Like one that wants to catch a train,
Or wrestles with internal pain?
Because he finds his egg contain –
Green, hungry, horrible and plain –
    An Infant Crocodile.

               Hilaire Belloc: *Cautionary Verses*

SLAP-UP DINNERS

Christmas goose and Christmas pudding

His active little crutch was heard upon the floor, and back came Tiny Tim before another word was spoken, escorted by his brother and sister to his stool before the fire; and while Bob, turning up his cuffs – as if, poor fellow, they were capable of being made more shabby – compounded some hot mixture in a jug with gin and lemons, and stirred it round and round and put it on the hob to simmer; Master Peter, and the two ubiquitous young Cratchits went to fetch the goose, with which they soon returned in high procession.

Such a bustle ensued that you might have thought a goose the rarest of all birds; a feathered phenomenon, to which a black swan was a matter of course; and in truth it was something very like it in that house. Mrs Cratchit made the gravy (ready beforehand in a little saucepan) hissing hot; Master Peter mashed the potatoes with incredible vigour; Miss Belinda sweetened up the apple-sauce; Martha dusted the hot plates; Bob took Tiny Tim beside him in a tiny corner at the table; the two young Cratchits set chairs for everybody, not forgetting themselves, and mounting guard upon their posts, crammed spoons into their mouths, lest they should shriek for goose before their turn came to be helped. At last the dishes were set on, and grace was said. It was succeeded by a breathless pause, as Mrs Cratchit, looking slowly all along the carving-knife, prepared to plunge it in the breast; but when she did, and when the long expected gush of stuffing issued forth, one murmur of delight arose all round the board, and even Tiny Tim, excited by the two young Cratchits, beat on the table with the handle of his knife, and feebly cried Hurrah!

There never was such a goose. Bob said he didn't believe there ever was such a goose cooked. Its tenderness and flavour, size and cheapness, were the themes of universal admiration. Eked out by the apple-sauce and mashed potatoes, it was a sufficient dinner for the whole family; indeed, as Mrs Cratchit said with great delight (surveying one small atom of a bone upon the dish), they hadn't ate it all at last! Yet every one had had enough, and the youngest Cratchits in particular, were steeped in sage and onion to the eybrows! But now, the plates being changed by Miss Belinda, Mrs Cratchit left the room alone – too nervous to bear witnesses – to take the pudding up, and bring it in.

Suppose it should not be done enough! Suppose it should break in turning out! Suppose somebody should have got over the wall of the back-yard, and stolen it, while they were merry with the goose: a supposition at which the two young Cratchits became livid! All sorts of horrors were supposed.

Hallo! A great deal of steam! The pudding was out of the copper. A smell like a washing-day! That was the cloth. A smell like an eating-house, and a pastry cook's next door to each other, with a laundress's next door to that! That was the pudding. In half a minute Mrs Cratchit entered: flushed, but smiling proudly: with the pudding, like a speckled cannon-ball, so hard and firm, blazing in half of half-a-quartern of ignited brandy, and bedight with Christmas holly stuck into the top.

Oh, a wonderful pudding! Bob Cratchit said, and calmly too, that he regarded it as the greatest success achieved by Mrs Cratchit since their marriage. Mrs Cratchit said that now the weight was off her mind, she would confess she had had her doubts about the quantity of flour. Everybody had something to say about it, but nobody said or thought it was at all a small pudding for a large family. It would have been flat heresy to do so. Any Cratchit would have blushed to hint at such a thing.

At last the dinner was all done, the cloth was cleared, the hearth swept, and the fire made up. The compound in the jug being tasted, and considered perfect, apples and oranges were put upon the table, and a shovel-full of chestnuts on the fire. Then all the Cratchit family drew round the hearth, in what Bob Cratchit called a circle, meaning half a one; and at Bob Cratchit's elbow stood the family display of glass; two tumblers, and a custard-cup without a handle.

These held the hot stuff from the jug, however, as well as golden goblets would have done; and Bob served it out with beaming looks, while the chestnuts on the fire sputtered and crackled noisily. Then Bob proposed:

'A Merry Christmas to us all, my dears. God bless us!'

Which all the family re-echoed.

'God bless us every one!' said Tiny Tim, the last of all.

Charles Dickens: *A Christmas Carol*

Dinner is sarved!

'Dinner is sarved!' at length exclaimed the stiff-necked foot-boy advancing into the centre of the room, extending his right arm like a guide-post. He then wheeled out, and placed himself at the head of a line of servants, formed by the gentleman Mr Jorrocks had seen in the yard; a square-built old man, in the Muleygrubs livery of a coachman; Mr De Green's young man in pepper-and-salt, with black velveteens; and Mr Slowan's ditto, in some of his master's old clothes. These lined the baronial hall, through which the party passed to the dining-room. Muleygrubs (who was now attired in a Serjeant's coat, with knee-buckled breeches and black silk stockings) offered his arm to Mrs Slowan, Mr De Green took Miss Slowan, the Professor paired off with Miss De Green, and Mr Jorrocks brought up the rear with Mrs Muleygrubs, leaving Jacob Jones and Mr Slowan to follow at their leisure. This party of ten was the result of six-and-twenty invitations.

'Vot, you've *three* o' these poodered puppies, have you?' observed Mr Jorrocks, as they passed along the line; adding, 'You come it strong!'

'We can't do with less,' replied the lady, the cares of dinner strong upon her.

'*Humph!* Well, I doesn't know 'bout that,' grunted Mr Jorrocks forcing his way up the room, seizing and settling himself into a chair on his hostess' right; 'Well, I doesn't know 'bout that,' repeated he, arranging his napkin over his legs, 'women waiters agin the world, say I! I'll back our Batsay, big and 'ippy as she is, to beat any two fellers at waitin'.'

Mrs Muleygrubs, anxious as she was for the proper arrangement of her guests, caught the purport of the foregoing, and, woman-like, darted a glance of ineffable contempt at our friend.

Our Master, seeing he was not likely to find a good listener at this interesting moment, proceeded to reconnoitre the room, and make mental observations on the unaccustomed splendour.

The room was a blaze of light. Countless compos swealed and simmered in massive gilt candelabras, while ground lamps of various forms lighted up the salmon-coloured walls, brightening the countenances of many ancestors, and exposing the dullness of the ill-cleaned plate.

The party having got shuffled into their places, the Rev Jacob Jones said an elaborate grace, during which the company stood.

'I'll tell you a rum story about grace,' observed Mr Jorrocks to Mrs Muleygrubs, as he settled himself into his seat, and spread his napkin over his knees. 'It 'appened at Croydon. The landlord o' the Grey'ound told a wise waiter, when the Duke axed 'im a question, always to say Grace. According the Duke o' Somebody, in changin' osses, popped his 'ead out o' the chay, and inquired wot o'clock it was. – "For wot we're a goin' to receive the Lord make us truly thankful," replied the waiter.'

Mrs Muleygrubs either did not understand the story, or was too intent upon other things; at all events, Mr Jorrocks's *haw! haw! haw!* was all that greeted its arrival. – But to dinner.

There were two soups – at least two plated tureens, one containing pea-soup, the other mutton-broth. Mr Jorrocks said he didn't like the latter, it always reminded him of 'a cold in the 'ead'. The pea-soup he thought werry like oss-gruel; – that he kept to himself.

'Sherry or *My*-dearer?' inquired the stiff-necked boy, going round with a decanter in each hand, upsetting the soup-spoons, and dribbling the wine over people's hands.

While these were going round, the coachman and Mr De Green's boy entered with two dishes of fish. On removing the large plated covers, six pieces of skate and a large haddock made their appearance. Mr Jorrocks's countenance fell five-and-twenty per cent., as he would say. He very soon despatched one of the six pieces of skate, and was just done in time to come in for the tail of the haddock.

'The Duke 'ill come on badly for fish, I'm thinkin',' said Mr Jorrocks, eyeing the empty dishes as they were taken off.

'Oh, Marmaduke don't eat fish,' replied Mrs M.

'Oh, I doesn't mean your Duke, but the Duke o' Rutland,' rejoined Mr Jorrocks.

Mrs Muleygrubs didn't take.

'Nothin' left for *Manners*, I mean, mum,' explained Mr Jorrocks, pointing to the empty dish.

Mrs Muleygrubs smiled, because she thought she ought, though she did not know why.

'Sherry or My-dearer, sir?' inquired the stiff-necked boy, going his round as before.

Mr Jorrocks asked Mrs Muleygrubs to take wine, and having satisfied himself that the sherry was bad, he took My-dearer, which was worse.

'Bad ticket, I fear,' observed Mr Jorrocks aloud to himself, smacking his lips. 'Have ye any swipes?'

'Sober-water and Seltzer-water,' replied the boy.

''Ang your sober-water!' growled Mr Jorrocks.

'Are you a hard rider, Mr Jorrocks?' now asked his hostess, still thinking anxiously of her dinner.

'*Ardest in England*, mum,' replied our friend confidently, muttering aloud to himself, 'may say that, for I never goes off the 'ard road if I can 'elp it.'

After a long pause, during which the conversation gradually died out, a kick was heard at the door, which the stiff-necked foot-boy having replied to by opening, the other boy appeared, bearing a tray, followed by all the other flunkeys, each carrying a silver-covered dish.

'Come *that's* more like the thing,' said Mr Jorrocks aloud to himself, eyeing the procession.

A large dish was placed under the host's nose, another under that of Mrs Muleygrubs.

'Roast beef and boiled turkey?' said Mr Jorrocks to himself, half inclined to have a mental bet on the subject. 'May be saddle o' mutton and chickens,' continued he, pursuing the speculation.

Four T. Cox Savory side-dishes, with silver rims and handles, next took places, and two silver-covered china centre dishes completed the arrangement.

'You've lots o' plate,' observed Mr Jorrocks to Mrs Muleygrubs, glancing down the table.

'Can't do with less,' replied the lady.

Stiffneck now proceeded to uncover, followed by his comrade. He began at his master, and, giving the steam-begrimed cover a flourish in the air, favoured his master's bald head with a hot shower-bath. Under pretence of admiring the pattern, Mr Jorrocks had taken a peep under the side-dish before him, and seeing boiled turnips, had settled that there was a round of beef at the bottom of the table. Spare ribs presented themselves to view. Mrs Muleygrubs's dish held a degenerate turkey, so lean and so lank that it looked as if it had been starved instead of fed. There was a rein-deer tongue under one centre dish, and sausages under the other. Minced veal, forbidding-looking *Rissoles*, stewed celery, and pigs' feet occupied the corner dishes.

'God bless us! what a dinner!' ejaculated Mr Jorrocks, involuntarily.

R. S. Surtees: *Handley Cross*

A College feast

The wall lights in the hall were turned off for the feast, and the tables were lit by candles. The candle light shone on silver salts, candlesticks, great ornamental tankards, and on gold cups and plates, all arranged down the middle of the tables. Silver and gold shone under the flickering light; as one looked above the candlesticks, the linenfold was half in darkness and the roof was lost.

In order to seat Sir Horace as Chrystal insisted, Winslow had been brought down from the high table, and so had Pilbrow and Pilbrow's French writer. I sat opposite Winslow and started to talk across the table to the Frenchman. He was, as it turned out, very disappointing.

I recalled the excitement with which I heard Pilbrow was bringing him, and the cultural snobbery with which we had piqued Chrystal and dismissed Sir Horace. How wrong we were. An evening by Sir Horace's side would have been far more rewarding.

The Frenchman sat stolidly while Pilbrow had a conversational fling. 'Pornograms,' Pilbrow burst out. 'An absolutely essential word – Two meanings. Something written, as in telegram. Something drawn, as in diagram.' The Frenchman was not amused, and went on talking like a passage from his own books.

But, if he did not enjoy himself, others made up for it. All through the feast we heard a commentary from Gay, who sat at the end of the high table, not far away from us.

'Oysters? Excellent. You never did relish oysters, did you, Despard? Waiter, bring me Mr Despard-Smith's oysters. Capital. I remember having some particularly succulent oysters in Oxford one night when they happened to be giving me an honorary degree. Do you know, those oysters slipped down just as though they were taking part in the celebration.'

He did not follow our modern fashion in wines. Champagne was served at feasts, but it had become the habit to pass it by and drink the hocks and moselles instead. Not so Gay. 'There's nothing like a glass of champagne on a cold winter night. I've always felt better for a glass of champagne. Ah. Let me see, I've been coming to these feasts now for getting on for sixty years. I'm happy to say I've never missed a feast through illness, and I've always enjoyed my glass of champagne.'

He kept having his glass filled, and addressed not only the end of his own table, but also ours.

'My saga-men never had a meal like this. Grand old Njal never had such a meal. My saga-men never had a glass of champagne. It was a very hard, dark, strenuous life those men lived, and they weren't afraid to meet their fates. Grand chaps they were. I'm glad I've been responsible for making thousands of people realise what grand chaps they were. Why, when I came on the scene, they were almost unknown in this country. And now, if a cultivated man does not know as much about them as he knows about the heroes of the Iliad, he's an ignoramus. You hear that, Despard? You hear that, Eustace? I repeat, he's an ignoramus.'

We sat a long time over the port and claret, the fruit and coffee and cigars. There were no speeches at all. At last – it was nearly half-past ten – we moved into the combination room again. Roy Calvert was starting some concealed badinage at the expense of Crawford and Despard-Smith. Like everyone else, he was rosy, bright-eyed, and full of well being. Like everyone except Nightingale, that is: Nightingale had brought no guest, was indifferent to food, and always hated drinking or seeing others drink. He stood in the crush of the combination room, looking strained in the midst of the elation. Winslow came up to Gay, who was making his way slowly – the press of men parted in front of him – to his special chair.

'Ah, Winslow. What a magnificent feast this has been!'

'Are you going to congratulate me on it?' asked Winslow.

'Certainly not,' said Gay. 'You gave up being Steward a great number of years ago. I shall congratulate the man responsible for this excellent feast. Getliffe is our present steward. That's the man. Where is Getliffe? I congratulate him. Splendid work these young scientists do, splendid.'

C. P. Snow: *The Masters*

Dining with the Bishop

SEP 4. 1783. . . . About 1. o'clock Mr and Mrs Custance called here in their Coach and took me with them to Norwich to dine with the Bishop. I was dressed in a Gown and Cassock and Scarf. We got there to the Palace abt. 3 o'clock, and there dined and spent the Afternoon with his Lordship Dr Bagot, and his Lady Mrs Bagot, whose Name before Marriage was Miss Hay, the two Miss Hay's her Sisters, two Mr Hay's her Brothers, a Mr Gooch the Bishop's Chaplain, Dr Brook of Yarmouth, Mr Buxton of Easton, and his Nephew the Revd Mr Buxton, Mr Du Quesne, Mr Priest of Reepham, and 5 strange Clergymen. There were 20 of us at the Table and a very elegant Dinner the Bishop gave us. We had 2 Courses of 20 Dishes each Course, and a Desert after of 20 Dishes. Madeira, red and white Wines. The first Course amongst many other things were 2 Dishes of prodigious fine stewed Carp and Tench, and a fine Haunch of Venison. Amongst the second Course a fine Turkey Poult, Partridges, Pidgeons and Sweatmeats. Desert – amongst other things,

Mulberries, Melon, Currants, Peaches, Nectarines and Grapes. A most beautiful Artificial Garden in the Center of the Table remained at Dinner and afterwards, it was one of the prettiest things I ever saw, about a Yard long, and about 18 Inches wide, in the middle of which was a high round Temple supported on round Pillars, the Pillars were wreathed round with artificial Flowers – on one side was a Shepherdess on the other a Shepherd, several handsome Urns decorated with artificial Flowers also &c. &c. The Bishop behaved with great affability towards me as I remembered him at Christ Church in Oxford. He was also very affable and polite to all the Clergy present. Mr and Mrs Custance were exceedingly pleased, with both Bishop and Mrs Bagot, as seemed everybody else. About half past 6.o'clock we all withdrew from the dining Room to the Library or Drawing Room, where we had Tea and Coffee brought round to each of us.

James Woodforde: *The Diary of a Country Parson*

A grand blow-out

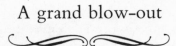

The ladies, imprisoned in their bodices, had their hair so plastered down with pommade that it reflected the light, while the men sat well away from the table, puffing out their chests and sticking out their elbows for fear of getting anything on their coats.

Coo, what a hole they made in that veal! If there was very little talk there was a mighty lot of chewing. The salad-bowl was emptying and a spoon stood upright in the thick sauce, a rich yellow sauce that looked like a jelly. In it they fished for bits of veal, and there still were some, so the bowl passed from hand to hand and faces looked down, hunting for mushrooms. The big loaves of bread standing against the wall behind the guests seemed to be melting away. Between mouthfuls came the sound of glasses being put down again on the table. The sauce was a bit on the salt side and so four bottles were needed to drown this blessed veal, which slipped down like a

custard and turned your insides into a fiery furnace. And then, before
you had time to breathe, enter the stewed chine of pork in a deep
dish and surrounded with big boiled potatoes, enveloped in a cloud
of steam. A shout went up: blimey, this was a bit of all right!
Everybody liked this. Now they really were going to get up an
appetite, and everyone cast sidelong glances at the dish and cleaned
his knife on his bread so as to be ready. Then when they had helped
themselves they dug each other in the ribs and talked with their
mouths full. Wasn't it scrumptious, this pork! Soft, yet solid, and
you could feel it slipping down the whole length of your innards
right to your feet! The potatoes were a dream. It wasn't at all salt,
but just on account of the potatoes it required a bit of irrigating every
minute. Four more bottles were killed. The plates were wiped so
clean that they did again for the peas and bacon. Ah well, vegetables
didn't take up any room, and you could put that away in ladlefuls
just for fun. A real feast, ladies' pleasure, as you might say. The best
thing about the peas was the bits of bacon, fried to a turn and stinking
like horses' hooves. Two bottles did for that.

'Mum, Mum!' Nana called, 'Augustine's putting her hands in my
plate!'

'Oh, shut up, do! Why don't you hit her?' answered Gervaise with
her mouth full of peas.

In the next room Nana was presiding over the children's table. She
was sitting next to Victor and had put her brother Étienne next to
little Pauline. In this way they could play at being grown-ups, two
married couples having a dinner party. At first Nana had served her
guests very genteelly, with the polite smiles of a lady, but then she
had given in to her passion for bacon and had collared all the bits for
herself. Boss-eyed Augustine, who was prowling craftily round the
kids, took advantage of this and seized handfuls of bacon on the
pretext of sharing the bits out more fairly. Nana flew into a rage and
bit her wrist.

'All right,' muttered Augustine, 'then I shall tell your mother that
after the veal you told Victor to kiss you.'

But everything settled down again because Gervaise and Ma
Coupeau came in to take up the goose. At the grown-up table
they were having a breather, sitting back on their chairs. The men
unbuttoned their waistcoats and the ladies dabbed their faces with
their napkins. It made a sort of interval in the meal, and only one or

two of them went on chewing and swallowing large mouthfuls of bread without realising they were doing so. They were just waiting and letting their food settle. Night had slowly fallen, and a dreary, ashen greyness was deepening behind the curtains. When Augustine set down two lighted lamps, one at each end, the bright light showed up the state the table was in, with dirty plates and forks, and wine-stains and crumbs all over the cloth. In spite of the strong smell rising all round, their noses turned towards the kitchen, drawn by certain whiffs of hot air.

'Can I give you a hand?' inquired Virginie.

She jumped from her chair and went into the other room, followed by all the other women. They stood round the roaster and gazed with rapt attention at Gervaise and Ma Coupeau as they tugged away at the bird. Then a clamour arose in which could be heard screams of joy and jumps of excitement from the children. There was a triumphal procession back to the other room, with Gervaise carrying the goose, arms held out stiff, face streaming with perspiration, beaming and speechless, the women walking behind, also grinning, whilst Nana, bringing up the rear, goggled as she stood on tiptoe to see. When the goose was on the table, huge, golden brown and anointed with gravy, they did not attack it straight away. The whole company was struck dumb with awe and respectful amazement, and comments were exchanged with blinkings of eyes and noddings of heads. Lumme, what a bird! What legs! What a breast!

'That one didn't fatten itself by licking the wall,' opined Boche.

Thereupon they went into details about it. Gervaise gave the precise facts: it was the finest bird she could find at the poulterer's in the Faubourg Poissonnière; it weighed twelve and a half pounds on the coal merchant's scales, it had taken a whole bag of coal to cook it and she had just got three basins of fat out of it. Virginie chipped in to boast of having seen the bird before it was cooked, and you could have eaten it like that, she said, so fine and white was the skin, a real blonde's skin, you know. All the men laughed and smacked their lips with sexy greed. Except Lorilleux and his wife who sniffed, outraged at seeing such a bird on Clip-Clop's table.

'Well, come on, we aren't going to swallow it whole!' Gervaise said eventually. 'Who's going to carve? . . . oh no, not me! It's too big, it quite frightens me.'

Coupeau volunteered. Dammit, it was quite simple, all you had to do was to grab hold of the limbs and pull; the pieces would be just as good to eat. But there was a chorus of protest and the carving knife was taken away from him; no, when he carved he turned the dish into a real charnel-house. For a moment they looked round for a willing man. Then Madame Lerat said sweetly:

'Listen, it should be Monsieur Poisson . . . yes, certainly Monsieur Poisson.'

As the company didn't seem to see why, she added in even more honeyed tones:

'Of course it should be Monsieur Poisson because he knows all about weapons.'

And she handed over the knife she was holding to the policeman. The whole table laughed with relief and approval. Poisson bowed with military stiffness and moved the goose over in front of him. His neighbours, Gervaise and Madame Boche, shifted to one side to give him plenty of elbow-room. He carved slowly, with sweeping movements and with his eyes fixed on the bird as though to nail it to the dish. As he buried the knife in the crackling carcase Lorilleux exclaimed in a burst of patriotic fervour:

'Supposing it was a Cossack, eh?'

'Did you ever fight any Cossacks, Monsieur Poisson?' inquired Madame Boche.

'No, only Bedouins,' answered the policeman, detaching a wing. 'There aren't any Cossacks left.'

A heavy silence fell. All necks were craned and all eyes followed the knife. Poisson was keeping a surprise up his sleeve. Suddenly he made the last stroke, and the rear of the creature came away and stood up, rump in the air: it was the bishop's mitre. There was a burst of admiration. Nothing like old soldiers for parlour tricks! But meanwhile the goose had discharged a jet of gravy from the gaping hole in its rear, which gave Boche a chance for a witticism:

'I'll sign on if someone will pee into my mouth like that!'

'Oh, the dirty old man!' exclaimed the ladies. 'Isn't he filthy!'

'No, I don't know anybody so disgusting,' said his wife, angrier than the others. 'Shut up, will you! You're enough to make an army sick. You know he's doing it so as to get the lot for himself.'

At this point Clémence repeated insistently above the din:

'Monsieur Poisson, listen, Monsieur Poisson, you will save the rump for me, won't you?'

'My dear, the rump is yours by right,' said Madame Lerat in her most discreetly suggestive tone.

By now the goose was all carved up. The policeman, having let the company admire the bishop's mitre for a few moments, had placed the pieces round the dish so that people could help themselves. But the ladies were complaining about the heat and undoing their dresses. Coupeau shouted that they were in their own home, so balls to the neighbours! And he threw open the street door so that the party went on to the rumble of passing cabs and the tramp of passers-by. Now, with their jaws a bit rested and a new gap in their stomachs, they resumed their dinner and fell upon the goose with furious energy. The mere fact of waiting and watching the goose being carved, observed the facetious Boche, had sent the veal and the pork right down into his legs.

It was a grand blow-out, and no mistake!

Emile Zola: *L'Assommoir* (translated by Leonard Tancock)

Noble and enough

13 January 1663: My poor wife rose by five o'clock in the morning, before day, and went to market and bought fowls and many other things for dinner, with which I was highly pleased; and the chine of beef was down also before six o'clock, and my own jack, of which I was doubtful, do carry it very well. Things being put in order, and the cook come, I went to the office, where we sat till noon and then broke up, and I home; whither by and by comes Dr Clerke and his lady, his sister and a she-cousin, and Mr Pierce and his wife; which was all my guests. I had for them, after oysters, at first course a hash of rabbits, a lamb and a rare chine of beef. Next a great dish of roasted fowl, cost me about 30s., and a tart; then fruit and cheese. My dinner was noble and enough. I had my house mighty clean and neat; my room below with a good fire in it; my dining room above, and my chamber being made a withdrawing-chamber; and my wife's a good

fire also. After dinner the women to cards in my wife's chamber, and the Dr and Mr Pierce in mine, because the dining-room smokes unless I keep a good charcoal fire, which I was not then provided with. At night to supper, had a good sack posset and cold meat, and sent my guests away about ten o'clock at night, both them and myself highly pleased with our management of this day; and indeed their company was very fine, and Mrs Clerke a very witty, fine lady, though a little conceited and proud. So weary, so to bed. I believe this day's feast will cost me near £5.

Samuel Pepys: *Diary*

A Dublin Christmas

A fat brown goose lay at one end of the table, and at the other end, on a bed of creased paper strewn with sprigs of parsley, lay a great ham, stripped of its outer skin and peppered over with crust crumbs, a neat paper frill round its shin, and beside this was a round of spiced beef. Between these rival ends ran parallel lines of side-dishes: two little minsters of jelly, red and yellow; a shallow dish full of blocks of blancmange and red jam, a large green leaf-shaped dish with a stalk-shaped handle, on which lay bunches of purple raisins and peeled almonds, a companion dish on which lay a solid rectangle of Smyrna figs, a dish of custard topped with grated nut meg, a small bowl full of chocolates and sweets wrapped in gold and silver papers and a glass vase in which stood some tall celery stalks. In the centre of the table there stood, as sentries to a fruit-stand which upheld a pyramid of oranges and American apples, two squat old-fashioned decanters of cut glass, one containing port and the other dark sherry. On the closed square piano a pudding in a huge yellow dish lay in waiting, and behind it were three squads of bottles of stout and ale and minerals, drawn up according to the colours of their uniforms, the first two black, with brown and red labels, the third and smallest squad white, with transverse green sashes.

Gabriel took his seat boldly at the head of the table and, having looked to the edge of the carver, plunged his fork firmly into the goose. He felt at ease now, for he was an expert carver and liked nothing better than to find himself at the head of a well-laden table.

'Miss Furlong, what shall I send you?' he asked. 'A wing or a slice of the breast?'

'Just a small slice of the breast.'

'Miss Higgins, what for you?'

'O, anything at all, Mr Conroy.'

While Gabriel and Miss Daly exchanged plates of goose and plates of ham and spiced beef, Lily went from guest to guest with a dish of hot floury potatoes wrapped in a white napkin. This was Mary Jane's idea and she had also suggested apple sauce for the goose, but Aunt Kate had said that plain roast goose without any apple sauce had always been good enough for her and she hoped she might never eat worse. Mary Jane waited on her pupils and saw that they got the best slices, and Aunt Kate and Aunt Julia opened and carried across from the piano bottles of stout and ale for the gentlemen and bottles of minerals for the ladies. There was a great deal of confusion and laughter and noise, the noise of orders and counter-orders, of knives and forks, of corks and glass-stoppers. Gabriel began to carve second helpings as soon as he had finished the first round without serving himself. Every one protested loudly, so that he compromised by taking a long draught of stout, for he had found the carving hot work. Mary Jane settled down quietly to her supper, but Aunt Kate and Aunt Julia were still toddling round the table, walking on each other's heels, getting in each other's way and giving each other unheeded orders. Mr Browne begged of them to sit down and eat their suppers and so did Gabriel, but they said there was time enough, so that, at last Freddy Malins stood up and, capturing Aunt Kate, plumped her down on her chair amid general laughter.

When every one had been well served Gabriel said, smiling:

'Now, if anyone wants a little more of what vulgar people call stuffing let him or her speak.'

A chorus of voices invited him to begin his own supper, and Lily came forward with three potatoes which she had reserved for him.

'Very well,' said Gabriel amiably, as he took another preparatory draught, 'kindly forget my existence, ladies and gentlemen, for a few minutes.' . . .

Gabriel having finished, the huge pudding was transferred to the table. The clatter of forks and spoons began again. Gabriel's wife served out spoonfuls of the pudding and passed the plates down the table. Midway down they were held up by Mary Jane, who replenished them with raspberry or orange jelly or with blancmange and jam. The pudding was of Aunt Julia's making, and she received praises for it from all quarters. She herself said that it was not quite brown enough.

'Well, I hope, Miss Morkan,' said Mr Browne, 'that I'm brown enough for you because, you know, I'm all brown.'

All the gentlemen, except Gabriel, ate some of the pudding out of compliment to Aunt Julia. As Gabriel never ate sweets the celery had been left for him. Freddy Malins also took a stalk of celery and ate it with his pudding. He had been told that celery was a capital thing for the blood and he was just then under doctor's care. Mrs Malins, who had been silent all through the supper, said that her son was going down to Mount Melleray in a week or so. The table then spoke of Mount Melleray, how bracing the air was down there, how hospitable the monks were and how they never asked for a penny-piece from their guests.

'And do you mean to say,' asked Mr Browne incredulously, 'that a chap can go down there and put up there as if it were a hotel and live on the fat of the land and then come away without paying anything?'

'O, most people give some donation to the monastery when they leave,' said Mary Jane.

'I wish we had an institution like that in our Church,' said Mr Browne candidly.

He was astonished to hear that the monks never spoke, got up at two in the morning and slept in their coffins. He asked what they did it for.

'That's the rule of the order,' said Aunt Kate firmly.

'Yes, but why?' asked Mr Browne.

Aunt Kate repeated that it was the rule, that was all. Mr Browne still seemed not to understand. Freddy Malins explained to him, as best he could, that the monks were trying to make up for the sins committed by all the sinners in the outside world. The explanation was not very clear, for Mr Browne grinned and said:

'I like that idea very much, but wouldn't a comfortable spring bed do them as well as a coffin?'

'The coffin' said Mary Jane, 'is to remind them of their last end.'

James Joyce: *Dubliners*

TRAVELLERS' FARE

Dinner at sea

It was midsummer in that glaring white town, and the heat was explosive. Some public holiday was in progress – could it have been the feast of St John the Baptist which marks the summer solstice? – and the waterfront was crowded with celebrating citizens in liquefaction. The excitement of a holiday and the madness of a heat wave hung in the air. The stone flags of the water's edge, where Joan and Xan Fielding and I sat down to dinner, flung back the heat like a casserole with the lid off. On a sudden, silent, decision we stepped down fully dressed into the sea carrying the iron table a few yards out and then our three chairs, on which, up to our waists in cool water, we sat round the neatly laid table-top, which now seemed by magic to be levitated three inches above the water. The waiter, arriving a moment later, gazed with surprise at the empty space on the quay; then, observing us with a quickly-masked flicker of pleasure, he stepped unhesitatingly into the sea, advanced waist deep with a butler's gravity, and, saying nothing more than 'Dinner-time', placed our meal before us – three beautifully grilled *kephali*, piping hot, and with their golden brown scales sparkling. To enjoy their marine flavour to the utmost, we dipped each by its tail for a second into the sea at our elbow . . . Diverted by this spectacle, the diners on the quay sent us can upon can of retsina till the table was crowded. A dozen boats soon gathered there, the craft radiating from the table's circumference like the petals of a marguerite. Leaning from their gently rocking boats, the fishermen helped us out with this sudden flux of wine, and by the time the moon and the Dog-Star rose over this odd symposium, a mandoline had appeared and *manga* songs in praise of hashish rose into the swooning night:

> 'When the hookah glows and bubbles,'
> wailed the fishermen;
> 'Brothers, not a word! Take heed!

'Behold the *mangas* all around us
'Puffing at the eastern weed . . .'

Patrick Leigh Fermor: *Mani*

Icelandic diet

Soups: Many of these are sweet and very unfortunate. I remember three with particular horror, one of sweet milk and hard macaroni, one tasting of hot marzipan, and one of scented hair oil. (But there is a good sweet soup, raspberry coloured, made of bilberry. L. M.)

Fish: Dried fish is a staple food in Iceland. This should be shredded with the fingers and eaten with butter. It varies in toughness. The tougher kind tastes like toe-nails, and the softer kind like the skin off the soles of one's feet.

In districts where salmon are caught, or round the coast, you get excellent fish, the grilled salmon particularly.

Meat: This is practically confined to mutton in various forms. The Danes have influenced Icelandic cooking, and to no advantage. Meat is liable to be served up in glutinous and half-cold lumps, covered with tasteless gravy. At the poorer farms you will only get Hángikyrl, *i.e.* smoked mutton. This is comparatively harmless when cold as it only tastes like soot, but it would take a very hungry man indeed to eat it hot . . .

Oddities

For the curious there are two Icelandic foods which should certainly be tried. One is Hákarl, which is half-dry, half-rotten shark. This is white inside with a prickly horn rind outside, as tough as an old boot. Owing to the smell it has to be eaten out of doors. It is shaved off with a knife and eaten with brandy. It tastes more like boot-polish than anything else I can think of. The other is Reyngi. This is the tail of the whale, which is pickled in sour milk for a year or so. If you intend to try it, do not visit a whaling station first. Incidentally, talking about pickling in sour milk, the Icelanders also do this to sheeps' udders, and the result is surprisingly very nice.

W. H. Auden and Louis MacNeice: *Letters from Iceland*

A Bedouin feast

. . . at last, two men came staggering through the thrilled crowd, carrying the rice and meat on a tinned copper tray or shallow bath, five feet across, set like a great brazier on a foot. In the tribe there was only this one food-bowl of the size, and an incised inscription ran round it in florid Arabic characters: 'To the glory of God, and in trust of mercy at the last, the property of His poor suppliant, Auda abu Tayi.' It was borrowed by the host who was to entertain us for the time; and, since my urgent brain and body made me wakeful, from my blankets in the first light I would see the dish going across country, and by marking down its goal would know where we were to feed that day.

The bowl was now brim-full, ringed round its edge by white rice in an embankment a foot wide and six inches deep, filled with legs and ribs of mutton till they toppled over. It needed two or three victims to make in the centre a dressed pyramid of meat such as honour prescribed. The centre-pieces were the boiled, upturned heads, propped on their severed stumps of necks, so that the ears, brown like old leaves, flapped out on the rice surface. The jaws gaped emptily upward, pulled open to show the hollow throat with the tongue, still pink, clinging to the lower teeth; and the long incisors whitely crowned the pile, very prominent above the nostrils' pricking hair and the lips which sneered away blackly from them.

This load was set down on the soil of the cleared space between us, where it steamed hotly, while a procession of minor helpers bore small cauldrons and copper vats in which the cooking had been done. From them, with much-bruised bowls of enamelled iron, they ladled out over the main dish all the inside and outside of the sheep; little bits of yellow intestine, the white tail-cushion of fat, brown muscles and meat and bristly skin, all swimming in the liquid butter and grease of the seething. The bystanders watched anxiously, muttering satisfactions when a very juicy scrap plopped out.

The fat was scalding. Every now and then a man would drop his baler with an exclamation, and plunge his burnt fingers, not reluctantly, in his mouth to cool them: but they persevered till at last their scooping rang loudly on the bottoms of the pots; and, with a gesture of triumph, they fished out the intact livers from their hiding place in the gravy and topped the yawning jaws with them.

Two raised each smaller cauldron and tilted it, letting the liquid splash down upon the meat till the rice-crater was full, and the loose grains at the edge swam in the abundance: and yet they poured, till, amid cries of astonishment from us, it was running over, and a little pool congealing in the dust. That was the final touch of splendour, and the host called us to come and eat.

We feigned a deafness, as manners demanded: at last we heard him, and looked surprised at one another, each urging his fellow to move first; till Nasir rose coyly, and after him we all came forward to sink on one knee round the tray, wedging in and cuddling up till the twenty-two for whom there was barely space were grouped around the food. We turned back our right sleeves to the elbow, and, taking lead from Nasir with a low 'In the name of God the merciful, the loving-kind', we dipped together.

The first dip, for me, at least, was always cautious, since the liquid fat was so hot that my unaccustomed fingers could seldom bear it: and so I would toy with an exposed and cooling lump of meat till others' excavations had drained my rice-segment. We would knead between the fingers (not soiling the palm), neat balls of rice and fat and liver and meat cemented by gentle pressure, and project them by leverage of the thumb from the crooked fore-finger into the mouth. With the right trick and the right construction the little lump held together and came clean off the hand; but when surplus butter and odd fragments clung, cooling, to the fingers, they had to be licked carefully to make the next effort slip easier away.

As the meat pile wore down (nobody really cared about rice: flesh was the luxury) one of the chief Howeitat eating with us would draw his dagger, silver hilted, set with turquoise, a signed masterpiece of Mohammed ibn Zari, of Jauf, and would cut criss-cross from the larger bones long diamonds of meat easily torn up between the fingers; for it was necessarily boiled very tender, since all had to be disposed of with the right hand which alone was honourable.

Our host stood by the circle, encouraging the appetite with pious ejaculations. At top speed we twisted, tore, cut and stuffed: never speaking, since conversation would insult a meal's quality, though it was proper to smile thanks when an intimate guest passed a select fragment, or when Mohammed el Dheilan gravely handed over a huge barren bone with a blessing. On such occasions I would return the compliment with some hideous impossible lump of guts, a flippancy which rejoiced the Howeitat, but which the gracious, aristocratic Nasir saw with disapproval.

At length some of us were nearly filled, and began to play and pick; glancing sideways at the rest till they too grew slow, and at last ceased eating, elbow on knee, the hand hanging down from the wrist over the tray edge to drip, while the fat, butter and scattered grains of rice cooled into a stiff white grease which gummed the fingers together. When all had stopped, Nasir meaningly cleared his throat, and we rose up together in haste with an explosive 'God requite it you, O host', to group ourselves outside among the tent-ropes while the next twenty guests inherited our leaving.

Those of us who were nice would go to the end of the tent where the flap of the roof-cloth, beyond the last poles, drooped down as an end curtain; and on this clan handkerchief (whose coarse goat-hair mesh was pliant and glossy with much use) would scrape the thickest of the fat from the hands. Then we would make back to our seats, and re-take them sighingly; while the slaves, leaving aside their portion, the skulls of the sheep, would come round our rank with a wooden bowl of water, and a coffee-cup as dipper, to splash over our fingers, while we rubbed them with the tribal soap-cake.

Meantime the second and third sittings by the dish were having their turn, and then there would be one more cup of coffee, or a glass of syrup-like tea; and at last the horses would be brought and we would slip out to them, and mount, with a quiet blessing to the hosts as we passed by. When our backs were turned the children would run in disorder upon the ravaged dish, tear our gnawed bones from one another, and escape into the open with valuable fragments to be devoured in security behind some distant bush; while the watchdogs of all the camp prowled round snapping, and the master of the tent fed the choicest offal to his greyhound.

T. E. Lawrence: *The Seven Pillars of Wisdom*

The dumpling

The coach went so slowly that by ten o'clock they had not covered twelve miles. The men got down three times to walk up hills. They were beginning to get worried, for they were to have lunched at Tôtes, and now there was no hope of getting there before dark. They were all looking out for an inn on the road, when the coach stuck in a snowdrift, and it took two hours to get it out.

Their spirits sank as their hunger increased; there was not anywhere they could get a bite or a sup, as the approach of the Prussians and the passage of the starving French troops had frightened alway all business. The gentlemen looked for food at the farms on the side of the road, but they could not even find any bread, as the suspicious peasants were hiding their stocks for fear of being robbed by the soldiers, who, having no rations, were forcibly requisitioning anything they found.

About one o'clock Loiseau announced that he had an aching void in his stomach. Everyone had been in the same condition for some time; and the longing for food, becoming more acute every minute, had killed conversation.

At intervals first one would yawn, then another. Each one in turn according to his character, his manners and his social position opened his mouth noisily or politely put his hand before the gaping, steaming chasm.

Boule de Suif bent down several times, as if feeling for something under her skirts. She hesitated a moment, looked at her neighbours, then quietly straightened herself. Everyone looked pale and drawn. Loiseau declared that he would give a thousand francs for a knuckle of ham. His wife made a sign of protest and then subsided. The mere mention of money wasted always worried her; she could not even see jokes on the subject. 'I admit I'm beginning to feel pretty rotten,' said the Comte. 'Why didn't I think of bringing food?'

Everyone was blaming himself for the same omission.

However, Cornudet had a flask of rum; he offered it round, but was met with a cold refusal. Loiseau alone accepted two sips, and as he handed back the flask, he expressed his thanks: 'Anyhow, it's good stuff; it warms one and takes the edge off one's hunger.' The alcohol cheered him up, and he suggested imitating the sailors in the lifeboat in the song and eating the fattest of the passengers. This indirect allusion to Boule de Suif shocked the more refined members of the party. There was a chilly silence; only Cornudet smiled. The two nuns had stopped mumbling over their rosaries, and, with their hands buried in their wide sleeves, were sitting motionless, keeping their eyes carefully on the ground, no doubt offering up to heaven the discomfort they were enduring.

At last at three o'clock, while they were in the middle of an interminable stretch of flat country, without a village in sight, Boule de Suif, bending down quickly, brought out from under the seat a large basket covered with a white napkin.

She took out first a small china plate and a slender silver drinking-cup, then a great pie-dish containing two whole chickens in aspic, ready carved; there were also visible in the basket other good things wrapped up – meat pies, preserved fruits and sweet biscuits, enough food for a three days' journey without having to rely on hotel meals: the necks of four bottles of wine protruded from the parcels of food. She took the wing of a chicken and began to eat it delicately with one of the small rolls called Regency rolls in Normandy.

Every eye was turned towards her. The smell of the food spread, tickling every nostril and making every mouth water, inducing a painful twitching of the muscles of the jaw under the ear. The ladies' contempt for the harlot increased in intensity, till they would have liked to kill her or throw her out of the coach into the snow, with her drinking-cup, her basket and her food.

But Loiseau could not take his eyes off the chicken-pie. He said: 'That's something like; Madame had more foresight than the rest of us! Some people always think of everything.' She glanced at him: 'Will you join me, Sir? It's no fun having nothing to eat since breakfast.' He bowed: 'I really can't refuse; I'm at the end of my tether. In Rome one must do as the Romans do, mustn't one, Madame?' And glancing round the coach, he added: 'At a moment like this one is glad to find a Good Samaritan.' He had a newspaper, which he spread out so as not to dirty his trousers, and on the point of a knife, which he always carried in his pocket, he speared a leg in its covering of jelly, stripped the meat off with his teeth and then ate it with such obvious relish that there was a great sigh of longing all round.

Thereupon Boule de Suif in a low respectful voice suggested to the nuns that they should share her repast. They both accepted unhesitatingly, and without raising their eyes began to eat very quickly, after stammering their thanks. Cornudet did not refuse his neighbour's offer either, and the two of them made a sort of table with the nuns by spreading newspapers over their knees.

Their mouths continued to open and shut, as they chewed and swallowed, attacking the food ravenously. Loiseau in his corner was making great efforts in a low voice to persuade his wife to follow suit. She refused for some time, but at last, unable to endure the agonies of emptiness, she gave way. Then her husband with formal politeness asked 'his charming neighbour' if he might offer his wife a mouthful; she replied with a pleasant smile: 'But of course, Sir, do,' and handed him the pie-dish.

An awkward moment occurred, when they had opened the first bottle of claret; there was only one drinking-cup. They passed it round after wiping it. Only Cornudet, no doubt out of mere politeness, put his lips on the place still wet from his neighbour's mouth.

Surrounded by the others eating and suffocated by the smell of food, the Comte and Comtesse de Bréville and M and Mme Carré-Lamadon suffered the excruciating torment associated with the name of Tantalus. Suddenly the manufacturer's young wife uttered a sigh, which made everyone turn round; she was as white as the snow outside. Her eyes closed and her head fell forward; she had fainted.

Her distracted husband appealed for help. No one knew what to do, till the elder of the two nuns, supporting the fainting lady's head, slipped Boule de Suif's drinking-cup between her lips and made her swallow a few drops of wine. The lady stirred, opened her eyes, smiled and declared in a weak voice that she was feeling quite well now. But, to prevent a repetition of the accident, the nun forced her to drink a cupful of claret, adding, 'It's nothing but hunger.'

Boule de Suif, getting very red and uncomfortable and looking at the four passengers who had eaten nothing, stammered: 'Really, if the ladies and gentlemen wouldn't mind my offering them something . . .' Then she stopped, fearing they would be insulted. Loiseau broke in: 'Dash it all, in a case like this we are all in the same boat, and we must pull together. Come, ladies, don't stand on ceremony; hang it all, accept her offer. Are we even sure of having a roof over our heads tonight? At our present pace we shan't get to Tôtes before midday to-morrow.' There was a pause; no one dared to take the responsibility of being the first to accept.

But the Comte settled the question. He turned to the fat, shy girl and said in his most impressive manner: 'We accept gratefully, Madame.'

It was only the first step that was difficult. The Rubicon once crossed, they set to heartily. The basket was emptied; it had still contained a *pâté de foie gras*, a lark pie, a piece of smoked tongue, some Bergamot pears, a slab of Pont-l'Évêque cheese, some fancy biscuits and a cupful of gherkins and pickled onions, for Boule de Suif, like all women, adored strong flavours.

They could not well eat the prostitute's food and not speak to her. So they began to talk, at first guardedly, then, as she showed admirable taste, they let themselves go more freely. Mme de Bréville and Mme Carré-Lamadon, whose manners were perfect, made themselves tactfully pleasant. The Comtesse in particular showed the affable condescension of the true patrician, proof against all vulgar contacts, and was charming. But the powerfully built Mme Loiseau, who had the soul of a policeman, remained surly, saying little and eating heartily.

They talked about the war, of course. They told stories of Prussian atrocities and deeds of French heroism; and all these people, who were bent on saving their own skins, paid tribute to the courage of others. Soon they got on to personal experiences, and Boule de Suif told, with unaffected emotion and that command of vigorous phrase which such girls often possess to express their primitive feelings, how she came to be leaving Rouen. 'I thought at first I should be able to stay,' she said. 'I had the house full of food, and I preferred to feed a few soldiers rather than leave home for some strange place. But, when I saw these Prussians, I couldn't stick it. Everything in me revolted, and I cried with shame all day. Oh! if only I were a man! I used to look at them out of the window, the fat swine in their spiked helmets, and my charwoman had to hold my hands to prevent my pitching the furniture out on to their heads. Then some were billeted on me; I went for the first one who came. They're no harder to strangle than anyone else! I'd have done for that one, if I hadn't been dragged off by the hair. After that I had to hide. At last I got a chance to leave Rouen, and here I am.'

She was warmly congratulated. She was going up in the estimation of her companions, who had not shown such courage; and Cornudet, as he listened, smiled with the benevolent approval of a Father of the Church . . .

Guy de Maupassant: *Boule de Suif*

STOKING UP

When you is married, you kin eat

The thought of her waist brought her back to practical matters. The green muslin measured seventeen inches about the waist, and Mammy had laced her for the eighteen-inch bombazine. Mammy would have to lace her tighter. She pushed open the door, listened and heard Mammy's heavy tread in the downstairs hall. She shouted for her impatiently, knowing she could raise her voice with impunity, as Ellen was in the smokehouse, measuring out the day's food to Cookie.

'Some folks thinks as how Ah kin fly,' grumbled Mammy, shuffling up the stairs. She entered puffing, with the expression of one who expects battle and welcomes it. In her large black hands was a tray upon which food smoked, two large yams covered with butter, a pile of buckwheat cakes dripping syrup, and a large slice of ham swimming in gravy. Catching sight of mammy's burden, Scarlett's expression changed from one of minor irritation to obstinate belligerency. In the excitement of trying on dresses she had forgotten Mammy's ironclad rule that, before going to any party, the O'Hara girls mut be crammed so full of food at home they would be unable to eat any refreshments at the party.

'It's no use. I won't eat it. You can just take it back to the kitchen.'

Mammy set the tray on the table and squared herself, hands on hips.

'Yas'm, you is! Ah ain' figgerin' on havin' happen whut happen at dat las' barbecue w'en Ah wuz too sick frum dem chittlins Ah et ter fetch you no tray befo' you went. You is gwine eat eve'y bite of dis.'

'I am not! Now, come here and lace me tighter because we are late already. I heard the carriage come round to the front of the house.'

Mammy's tone became wheedling.

'Now, Miss Scarlett, you be good an' come eat jes' a lil. Miss Carreen an' Miss Suellen done eat all dey'n.'

'They would,' said Scarlett contemptuously. 'They haven't any more spirit than a rabbit. But I won't! I'm through with trays. I'm not forgetting the time I ate a whole tray and went to the Calverts' and they had ice-cream out of ice they'd brought all the way from Savannah, and I couldn't eat but a spoonful. I'm going to have a good time to-day and eat as much as I please.'

At this defiant heresy, Mammy's brow lowered with indignation. What a young miss could do and what she could not do were as different as black and white in Mammy's mind; there was no middle ground of deportment between. Suellen and Carreen were clay in her powerful hands and harkened respectfully to her warnings. But it had always been a struggle to teach Scarlett that most of her natural impulses were unladylike. Mammy's victories over Scarlett were hard-won and represented guile unknown to the white mind.

'Ef you doan care 'bout how folks talks 'bout dis fambly, Ah does,' she rumbled. 'Ah ain' gwine stand by an' have eve'ybody at de pahty sayin' how you ain' fotched up right. Ah has tole you an' tole you dat you kin allus tell a lady by dat she eat lak a bird. An' Ah ain' aimin' ter have you go ter Mist' Wilkes' an' eat lak a fe'el han' an' gobble lak a hawg.'

'Mother is a lady and she eats,' countered Scarlett.

'W'en you is mahied, you kin eat, too,' retorted Mammy. 'W'en Miss Ellen yo' age, she never et nuthin' w'en she went out, an' needer yo' Aunt Pauline nor yo' Aunt Eulalie. An' dey all done mahied. Young misses whut eats heavy mos' gener'ly doan never ketch husbands.'

'I don't believe it. At that barbecue when you were sick and I didn't eat beforehand, Ashley Wilkes told me he *liked* to see a girl with a healthy appetite.'

Mammy shook her head ominously.

'Whut gempmums says an' whut dey thinks is two diffunt things. An' Ah ain' noticed Mist' Ashley axing fer ter mahy you.'

Scarlett scowled, started to speak sharply and then caught herself. Mammy had her there and there was no argument. Seeing the obdurate look on Scarlett's face, Mammy picked up the tray and, with the bland guile of her race, changed her tactics. As she started for the door, she sighed.

'Well'm, awright. Ah wuz tellin' Cookie w'ile she wuz a-fixin' dis tray, "You kin sho tell a lady by whut she *doan* eat," an' Ah say ter Cookie, "Ah ain' never seed no w'ite lady who et less'n Miss Melly

Hamilton did las' time she wuz visitin' Mist' Ashley" – Ah means, visitin' Miss India.'

Scarlett shot a look of sharp suspicion at her, but Mammy's broad face carried only a look of innocence and of regret that Scarlett was not the lady Melanie Hamilton was.

'Put down that tray and come lace me tighter,' said Scarlett irritably. 'And I'll try to eat a little afterwards. If I ate now I couldn't lace tight enough.'

Cloaking her triumph, Mammy set down the tray.

'Whut mah lamb gwine wear?'

'That,' answered Scarlett, pointing at the fluffy mass of green flowered muslin. Instantly Mammy was in arms.

'No, you ain'. It ain' fittin' fer mawnin'. You kain show yo' buzzum befo' three o'clock an' dat dress ain' got no neck an' no sleeves. An' you'll git freckled sho as you born, an' Ah ain' figgerin' on you gittin' freckled affer all de buttermilk Ah been puttin' on you all dis winter, bleachin' dem freckles you got at Savannah settin' on de beach. Ah sho gwine speak ter yo' Ma 'bout you.'

'If you say one word to her before I'm dressed I won't eat a bite,' said Scarlett coolly. 'Mother won't have time to send me back to change once I'm dressed.'

Mammy sighed resignedly, beholding herself outguessed. Between the two evils, it was better to have Scarlett wear an afternoon dress at a morning barbecue than to have her gobble like a hog.

'Hole onter sumpin' an' suck in yo' breaf,' she commanded.

Margaret Mitchell: *Gone with the Wind*

Fond of their food

Both old people, as is customary with old-world landowners, were extremely fond of their food. The moment it began to dawn (they were early risers) and the doors commenced their cacophonous recital, they would be seated at their table drinking coffee. After having his fill of coffee Afanasy Ivanovich would step out into the porch and flapping his handkerchief say: 'Shoo! Off the porch with you, geese!' His bailiff would usually attend him in the yard. He would then enter into conversation with him, asking him in great detail about his work, and making comments and giving orders which would have astounded anyone for the extraordinary knowledge of farming that they displayed, and no novice would ever even contemplate stealing anything from such a perspicacious master. But his bailiff was an old bird and he knew the right answers to make, and better still, he knew how to manage affairs.

After this Afanasy Ivanovich would return inside and approaching Pulcheria Ivanovna suggest: 'Well, Pulcheria Ivanovna, perhaps it's time for a little something to eat?'

'What would you like, Afanasy Ivanovich? Perhaps some short-cakes and bacon, or poppy seed rolls, or what about some salted mushrooms?'

'Well, perhaps I'll have some of the mushrooms, or maybe the rolls,' Afanasy Ivanovich would answer, and suddenly on the table there would appear a table cloth, laid with rolls and mushrooms.

An hour before lunch Afanasy Ivanovich would have another snack, downing a measure of vodka from an antique silver cup, chasing it with mushrooms, an assortment of dried fish and such like. They sat down to their lunch at twelve o'clock. In addition to the dishes and sauce boats the table groaned beneath a mass of jars with sealed lids, to stop the appetising aromas of old-world cooking escaping from them. The meat was usually accompanied by conversation on subjects of a prandial nature.

'It seems to me that this buckwheat,' Afanasy Ivanovich would begin, 'is a little burnt; would you not agree, Pulcheria Ivanovna?'

'No, Afanasy Ivanovich, try putting a little more butter in it and it won't appear burnt, or take some of this mushroom sauce in it.'

'Perhaps I will, too,' replied Afanasy Ivanovich, holding forward his plate: 'Let's see what it's like.'

After lunch, Afanasy Ivanovich would retire for an hour's nap, after which Pulcheria Ivanovna would bring him a sliced watermelon and say: 'Try this, Afanasy Ivanovich, such a good watermelon.'

'Just because it's red in the middle does not mean it's good, Pulcheria Ivanovna,' Afanasy Ivanovich would caution, taking a generous slice.

But the watermelon would be devoured without fail. After this Afanasy Ivanovich would eat a few more pears and set off for a walk around the garden in the company of Pulcheria Ivanovna. On their return to the house Pulcheria Ivanovna would set about her own affairs while her spouse sat outside on the porch, looking out into the garden, watching the pantry by turns revealing and concealing its interior, and the maids bumping into one another as they bore thither large quantities of God-knows-what in wooden crates, troughs, sieves and other fruit containers. After a little while he would send for Pulcheria Ivanovna or make his way to her himself and say: 'What could I have to eat, Pulcheria Ivanovna?'

'What would you like?' she would ask. 'Should I go and tell them to bring you the dumplings with cherries I specially had set aside for you?'

'That would be fine,' answered Afanasy Ivanovich.

'Or perhaps you'd like some jelly?'

'That would be rather good too,' replied Afanasy Ivanovich. Whereupon all this would be served up, and, as was right and proper, consumed.

Before supper Afanasy Ivanovich would partake of another little snack. Then at half past nine they would sit down to their supper. Directly after this they would retire to bed and silence would descend on this busy, but tranquil nook. The room in which Afanasy Ivanovich and Pulcheria Ivanovna slept, was so warm that few people would have been able to stand it for long. But Afanasy Ivanovich, for the sake of the extra warmth, even used to sleep on the stove, although the fierce heat often forced him to rise several times during the night and walk around the room. Occasionally, on these promenades about the room, Afanasy Ivanovich would emit groans.

This caused Pulcheria Ivanovna to ask: 'Why are you groaning, Afanasy Ivanovich?'

'The Lord only knows, Pulcheria Ivanovna, my stomach seems to be aching a little,' Afanasy Ivanovich replied.

'Perhaps you should have something to eat, Afanasy Ivanovich?'

'Well, I don't know, Pulcheria Ivanovna, is it a good idea? What is there to eat, in fact?'

'Some curds, or perhaps stewed pears in their juice?'

'Well, perhaps I will have a little taste,' said Afanasy Ivanovich.

A sleepy maid would be dispatched to forage in the cupboards and Afanasy Ivanovich would put away a plateful; after this he would usually announce: 'I do seem to feel a bit better now.'

Nikolai Gogol: *Old World Landowners*

Eating is unspiritual

'At this first dinner, George's partner was Emmeline. They talked of Nature. Emmeline protested that to her high mountains were a feeling and the hum of human cities torture. George agreed that the country was very agreeable, but held that London during the season also had its charms. He noticed with surprise and a certain solicitous distress that Miss Emmeline's appetite was poor, that it didn't, in fact exist. Two spoonfuls of soup, a morsel of fish, no bird, no meat, and three grapes – that was her whole dinner. He looked from time to time at her two sisters; Georgiana and Caroline seemed to be quite as abstemious. They waved away whatever was offered them with an expression of delicate disgust, shutting their eyes and averting their faces from the proffered dish, as though the lemon sole, the duck, the loin of veal, the trifle, were objects revolting to the sight and smell. George, who thought the dinner capital, ventured to comment on the sisters' lack of appetite.

'"Pray, don't talk to me of eating," said Emmeline, drooping like a sensitive plant. "We find it so coarse, so unspiritual, my sisters and I. One can't think of one's soul while one is eating."

'George agreed; one couldn't. "But one must live," he said.

'"Alas!" Emmeline sighed. "One must. Death is very beautiful, don't you think?" She broke a corner off a piece of toast and began to nibble at it languidly. "But since, as you say, one must live . . ." She made a little gesture of resignation. "Luckily a very little suffices to keep one alive." She put down her corner of toast half eaten.

'George regarded her with some surprise. She was pale, but she looked extraordinarily healthy, he thought; so did her sisters. Perhaps

240

if you were really spiritual you needed less food. He, clearly, was not spiritual.

'After this he saw them frequently. They all liked him, from Lady Lapith downwards. True, he was not very romantic or poetical; but he was such a pleasant, unpretentious, kind-hearted young man, that one couldn't help liking him. For his part, he thought them wonderful, wonderful, especially Georgiana. He enveloped them all in a warm, protective affection. For they needed protection; they were altogether too frail, too spiritual for this world. They never ate, they were always pale, they often complained of fever, they talked much and lovingly of death, they frequently swooned. Georgiana was the most ethereal of all; of the three she ate least, swooned most often, talked most of death, and was the palest – with a pallor that was so startling as to appear positively artificial. At any moment, it seemed, she might loose her precarious hold on this material world and become all spirit. To George the thought was a continual agony. If she were to die . . .

'She contrived, however, to live through the season, and that in spite of the numerous balls, routs, and other parties of pleasure which, in company with the rest of the lovely trio, she never failed to attend. In the middle of July the whole household moved down to the country. George was invited to spend the month of August at Crome.

'The house-party was distinguished; in the list of visitors figured the names of two marriageable young men of title. George had hoped that country air, repose, and natural surroundings might have restored to the three sisters their appetites and the roses of their cheeks. He was mistaken. For dinner, the first evening, Georgiana ate only an olive, two or three salted almonds, and half a peach. She was as pale as ever. During the meal she spoke of love.

'"True love," she said, "being infinite and eternal, can only be consummated in eternity. Indiana and Sir Rodolphe celebrated the mystic wedding of their souls by jumping into Niagara. Love is incompatible with life. The wish of two people who truly love one another is not to live together but to die together."

'"Come, come, my dear," said Lady Lapith, stout and practical. "What would become of the next generation, pray, if all the world acted on your principles?"

'"Mamma! . . ." Georgiana protested, and dropped her eyes.

'"In my young days," Lady Lapith went on, "I should have been laughed out of countenance if I'd said a thing like that. But then in my young days souls weren't as fashionable as they are now and we didn't think death was at all poetical. It was just unpleasant."

'"Mamma! . . ." Emmeline and Caroline implored in unison.

'"In my young days—" Lady Lapith was launched into her subject; nothing, it seemed, could stop her now. "In my young days, if you didn't eat, people told you you needed a dose of rhubarb. Nowadays . . ."

'There was a cry; Georgiana had swooned sideways on to Lord Timpany's shoulder. It was a desperate expedient; but it was successful. Lady Lapith was stopped.

'The days passed in an uneventful round of pleasures. Of all the gay party George alone was unhappy. Lord Timpany was paying his court to Georgiana, and it was clear that he was not unfavourably received. George looked on, and his soul was a hell of jealousy and despair. The boisterous company of the young men became intolerable to him; he shrank from them, seeking gloom and solitude. One morning, having broken away from them on some vague pretext, he returned to the house alone. The young men were bathing in the pool below; their cries and laughter floated up to him, making the quiet house seem lonelier and more silent. The lovely sisters and their mamma still kept their chambers; they did not customarily make their appearance till luncheon, so that the male guests had the morning to themselves. George sat down in the hall and abandoned himself to thought.

'At any moment she might die; at any moment she might become Lady Timpany. It was terrible, terrible. If she died, then he would die too; he would go to seek her beyond the grave. If she became Lady Timpany . . . ah, then! The solution of the problem would not be so simple. If she became Lady Timpany: it was a horrible thought. But then suppose she were in love with Timpany – though it seemed incredible that anyone could be in love with Timpany – suppose her life depended on Timpany, suppose she couldn't live without him? He was fumbling his way along this clueless labyrinth of suppositions when the clock struck twelve. On the last stroke, like an automaton released by the turning clockwork, a little maid, holding a large covered tray, popped out of the door that led from the kitchen regions into the hall. From his deep arm–chair George watched her (himself, it was evident, unobserved) with an idle curiosity. She pattered across the room and came to a halt in front of what seemed a blank expanse of panelling. She reached out her hand and, to George's extreme astonishment, a little door swung open, revealing the foot of a winding staircase. Turning sideways in order to get her tray through the narrow opening, the little maid darted in with a rapid crablike motion. The door closed behind her with a click. A minute later it opened again and the maid, without her tray, hurried back across the hall and disappeared in the direction of the kitchen. George tried to recompose his thoughts, but an invincible curiosity drew his mind towards the hidden door, the staircase, the little maid. It was in vain he told himself that the matter was none of his business, that to explore the secrets of that surprising door, that mysterious staircase within, would be a piece of unforgivable rudeness and indiscretion. It was in vain; for five minutes he struggled heroically with his curiosity, but at the end of that time he found himself standing in front of the innocent sheet of panelling through which the little maid had disappeared. A glance sufficed to show him the position of the secret door – secret, he perceived, only to those who looked with a careless eye. It was just an ordinary door let in flush with the panelling. No latch nor handle betrayed its position, but an unobtrusive catch sunk in the wood invited the thumb. George was astonished that he had not noticed it before; now he had seen it, it was so obvious, almost as obvious as the cupboard door in the library with its lines of imitation shelves and its dummy books. He pulled back the catch and peeped inside. The staircase, of which the degrees were made not of stone but of blocks of ancient oak, wound up and out of sight. A slit-like window admitted the daylight; he was at the foot of the central tower, and the little window looked out over the terrace; they were still shouting and splashing in the pool below.

'George closed the door and went back to his seat. But his curiosity was not satisfied. Indeed, this partial satisfaction had but whetted its appetite. Where did the staircase lead? What was the errand of the little maid? It was no business of his, he kept repeating – no business of his. He tried to read, but his attention wandered. A quarter-past twelve sounded on the harmonious clock. Suddenly determined, George rose, crossed the room, opened the hidden door, and began to ascend the stairs. He passed the first window, corkscrewed round, and came to another. He paused for a moment to look out; his heart beat uncomfortably, as though he were affronting some unknown danger. What he was doing, he told himself, was extremely ungentlemanly, horribly under-bred. He tiptoed onward and upward. One turn more, then half a turn, and a door confronted him. He halted before it, listened; he could hear no sound. Putting his eye to the keyhole, he saw nothing but a stretch of white sunlit wall. Emboldened, he turned the handle and stepped across the threshold. There he halted, petrified by what he saw, mutely gaping.

'In the middle of a pleasantly sunny little room – "it is now Priscilla's boudoir," Mr Wimbush remarked parenthetically – stood a small circular table of mahogany. Crystal, porcelain, and silver – all the shining apparatus of an elegant meal – were mirrored in its polished depths. The carcase of a cold chicken, a bowl of fruit, a great ham, deeply gashed to its heart of tenderest white and pink, the brown cannon ball of a cold plum-pudding, a slender Hock bottle, and a decanter of claret jostled one another for a place on this festive board. And round the table sat the three sisters, the three lovely Lapiths – eating!

'At George's sudden entrance they had all looked towards the door, and now they sat, petrified by the same astonishment which kept George fixed and staring. Georgiana, who sat immediately facing the door, gazed at him with dark, enormous eyes. Between the thumb and forefinger of her right hand she was holding a drumstick of the dismembered chicken; her little finger, elegantly crooked, stood apart from the rest of her hand. Her mouth was open, but the drumstick had never reached its destination; it remained, suspended, frozen, in mid-air. The other two sisters had turned round to look at the intruder. Caroline still grasped her knife and fork; Emmeline's fingers were round the stem of her claret glass. For what seemed a very long time, George and the three sisters stared at one another in silence. They were a group of statues. Then suddenly there was movement. Georgiana dropped her chicken bone, Caroline's knife and fork clattered on her plate. The movement propagated itself, grew more decisive; Emmeline sprang to her feet, uttering a cry. The wave of panic reached George; he turned and, mumbling something unintelligible as he went, rushed out of the room and down the winding stairs. He came to a standstill in the hall, and there, all by himself in the quiet house, he began to laugh.

'At luncheon it was noticed that the sisters ate a little more than usual. Georgiana toyed with some French beans and a spoonful of calves'-foot jelly. "I feel a little stronger to-day," she said to Lord Timpany, when he congratulated her on this increase of appetite; "a little more material," she added, with a nervous laugh. Looking up, she caught George's eye; a blush suffused her cheeks and she looked hastily away.

'In the garden that afternoon they found themselves for a moment alone.

'"You won't tell anyone, George? Promise you won't tell anyone," she implored. "It would make us look so ridiculous. And besides, eating *is* unspiritual, isn't it? Say you won't tell anyone."

'"I will," said George brutally. "I'll tell everyone, unless . . ."

'"It's blackmail."

'"I don't care," said George. "I'll give you twenty-four hours to decide."

'Lady Lapith was disappointed, of course; she had hoped for better things – for Timpany and a coronet. But George, after all, wasn't so bad. They were married at the New Year.'

Aldous Huxley: *Crome Yellow*

TABLE D'HÔTE

The summer nights

Every Friday five crates of oranges and lemons arrived from a fruiterer in New York – every Monday these same oranges and lemons left his back door in a pyramid of pulpless halves. There was a machine in the kitchen which could extract the juice of two hundred oranges in half an hour if a little button was pressed two hundred times by a butler's thumb.

At least once a fortnight a corps of caterers came down with several hundred feet of canvas and enough coloured lights to make a Christmas tree of Gatsby's enormous garden. On buffet tables, garnished with glistening hors-d'œuvre, spiced baked hams crowded against salads of harlequin designs and pastry pigs and turkeys bewitched to a dark gold. In the main hall a bar with a real brass rail was set up, and stocked with gins and liquors and with cordials so long forgotten that most of his female guests were too young to know one from another.

By seven o'clock the orchestra has arrived, no thin five-piece affair, but a whole pitful of oboes and trombones and saxophones and viols and cornets and piccolos, and low and high drums. The last swimmers have come in from the beach now and are dressing upstairs; the cars from New York are parked five deep in the drive, and already the halls and salons and verandas are gaudy with primary colours, and hair bobbed in strange new ways, and shawls beyond the dreams of Castile. The bar is in full swing, and floating rounds of cocktails permeate the garden outside, until the air is alive with chatter and laughter, and casual innuendo and introductions forgotten on the spot, and enthusiastic meetings between women who never knew each other's names.

F. Scott Fitzgerald: *The Great Gatsby*

The supreme sacrifice

I wasn't feeling any too good myself. From time to time in the course of this narrative I have had occasion to indicate my sentiments regarding Anatole, that peerless artist, and you will remember that the relative's account of how Sir Watkyn Bassett had basely tried to snitch him from her employment during his visit to Brinkley Court had shocked me to my foundations.

It is difficult, of course, to convey to those who have not tasted this wizard's products the extraordinary importance which his roasts and boileds assume in the scheme of things to those who have. I can only say that once having bitten into one of his dishes you are left with the feeling that life will be deprived of all its poetry and meaning unless you are in a position to go on digging in. The thought that Aunt Dahlia was prepared to sacrifice this wonder man merely to save a nephew from the cooler was one that struck home and stirred.

I don't know when I have been so profoundly moved. It was with a melting eye that I gazed at her. She reminded me of Sidney Carton.

'You were actually contemplating giving up Anatole for my sake?' I gasped.

'Of course.'

'Of course jolly well not! I wouldn't hear of such a thing.'

'But you can't go to prison.'

'I certainly can, if my going means that that supreme maestro will continue working at the old stand. Don't dream of meeting old Bassett's demands.'

'Bertie! Do you mean this?'

'I should say so. What's a mere thirty days in the second division? A bagatelle. I can do it on my head. Let Bassett do his worst. And,' I added in a softer voice, 'when my time is up and I come out into the world once more a free man, let Anatole do his best. A month of bread and water or skilly or whatever they feed you on in these establishments will give me a rare appetite. On the night when I emerge, I shall expect a dinner that will live in legend and song.'

'You shall have it.'

'We might be sketching out the details now.'

'No time like the present. Start with caviare? Or cantaloup?'

'And cantaloup. Followed by a strengthening soup.'

'Thick or clear?'

'Clear.'

'You aren't forgetting Anatole's *Velouté aux fleurs de courgette*?'

'Not for a moment. But how about his *Consommé aux Pommes d'Amour*?'

'Perhaps you're right.'

'I think I am. I feel I am.'

'I'd better leave the ordering to you.'

'It might be wisest.'

I took pencil and paper, and some ten minutes later I was in a position to announce the result.

'This, then,' I said, 'subject to such additions as I may think out in my cell, is the menu as I see it.'

And I read as follows:

Le Dîner

> *Caviare Frais*
> *Cantaloup*
> *Consommé aux Pommes d'Amour*
> *Sylphides à la crème d'écrevisses*
> *Mignonette de poulet petit Duc*
> *Points d'asperges à la Mistinguett*
> *Suprême de foie gras au champagne*
> *Neige aux Perles des Alpes*
> *Timbale de ris de veau Toulousaine*
> *Salade d'endive et de céleri*
> *Le Plum Pudding*
> *L'Etoile au Berger*
> *Benedictins Blancs*
> *Bombe Nero*
> *Friandises*
> *Diablotins*
> *Fruits*

'That about covers it, Aunt Dahlia?'

'Yes, you don't seem to have missed out much.'

'Then let's have the man in and defy him. Bassett!' I cried.

'Bassett!' shouted Aunt Dahlia.

'Bassett!' I bawled, making the welkin ring.

It was still ringing when he popped in, looking annoyed.

'What the devil are you shouting at me like that for?'

'Oh, there you are, Bassett.' I wasted no time in getting down to the agenda. 'Bassett, we defy you.'

The man was plainly taken aback. He threw a questioning look at Aunt Dahlia. He seemed to be feeling that Bertram was speaking in riddles.

'He is alluding,' explained the relative, 'to that idiotic offer of yours to call the thing off if I let you have Anatole. Silliest idea I ever heard. We've been having a good laugh about it. Haven't we, Bertie?'

'Roaring our heads off,' I assented.

He seemed stunned.

'Do you mean that you refuse?'

'Of course we refuse. I might have known my nephew better than to suppose for an instant that he would consider bringing sorrow and bereavement to an aunt's home in order to save himself unpleasant-ness. The Woosters are not like that, are they, Bertie?'

'I should say not.'

'They don't put self first.'

'You bet they don't.'

'I ought never to have insulted him by mentioning the offer to him. I apologise, Bertie.'

'Quite all right, old flesh and blood.'

She wrung my hand.

'Good night, Bertie, and good-bye – or, rather, *au revoir*. We shall meet again.'

'Absolutely. When the fields are white with daisies, if not sooner.'

'By the way, didn't you forget *Nonats de la Méditerranée au Fenouil?*'

'So I did. And *Selle d'Agneau aux laitues à la Greque*. Shove them on the charge sheet, will you?'

P. G. Wodehouse: *The Code of the Woosters*

The clean platter

Some singers sing of ladies' eyes,
And some of ladies' lips,
Refined ones praise their ladylike ways,
And coarse ones hymn their hips.
The *Oxford Book of English Verse*
Is lush with lyrics tender;
A poet, I guess, is more or less
Preoccupied with gender.
Yet I, though custom call me crude,
Prefer to sing in praise of food.

Food,
Yes, food,
Just any old kind of food.
Pheasant is pleasant, of course,
And terrapin, too, is tasty,
Lobster I freely endorse,
In pâté or patty or pasty.
But there's nothing the matter with butter,
And nothing the matter with jam,
And the warmest of greetings I utter
To the ham and the yam and the clam.
For they're food,
All food,
And I think very highly of food.
Though I'm broody at times
When bothered by rhymes,
I brood
On food.

Some painters paint the sapphire sea,
And some the gathering storm.
Others portray young lambs at play,

Table D'Hôte

But most, the female form.
'Twas trite in that primeval dawn
When painting got its start,
That a lady with her garments on
Is Life, but is she Art?
By undraped nymphs
I am not wooed;
I'd rather painters painted food.

Food,
Just food,
Just any old kind of food.
Go purloin a sirloin, my pet,
If you'd win a devotion incredible;
And asparagus tips vinaigrette,
Or anything else that is edible.
Bring salad or sausage or scrapple,
A berry or even a beet.
Bring an oyster, an egg, or an apple,
As long as it's something to eat.
If it's food,
It's food;
Never mind what kind of food.
When I ponder my mind
I consistently find
It is glued
On food.

Ogden Nash

Reviving Uncle George

I am not a man who speaks hastily in these matters. I weigh my words. And I say again that Anatole had surpassed himself. It was as good a dinner as I have ever absorbed, and it revived Uncle Thomas like a watered flower. As we sat down he was saying some things about the government which they wouldn't have cared to hear. With the *consommé pâté d'Italie* he said but what could you expect nowadays? With the *paupiettes de sole à la princesse* he admitted rather decently that the Government couldn't be held responsible for the rotten weather, anyway. And shortly after the *caneton Aylesbury à la broche* he was practically giving the lads the benefit of his whole-hearted support.

P. G. Wodehouse: *Carry on, Jeeves*

Ritual at Porterhouse

It was a fine Feast. No one, not even the Praelector who was so old he could remember the Feast of '09, could recall its equal – and Porterhouse is famous for its food. There was Caviar and Soupe à l'Oignon, Turbot au Champagne, Swan stuffed with Widgeon, and finally, in memory of the Founder, Beefsteak from an ox roasted whole in the great fireplace of the College Hall. Each course had a different wine and each place was laid with five glasses. There was Pouilly Fumé with the fish, champagne with the game and the finest burgundy from the College cellars with the beef. For two hours the silver dishes came, announced by the swish of the doors in the Screens as the waiters scurried to and fro, bowed down by the weight of the food and their sense of occasion. For two hours the members of Porterhouse were lost to the world, immersed in an ancient ritual that spanned the centuries. The clatter of knives and forks, the clink of glasses, the rustle of napkins and the shuffling feet of the College servants dimmed the present. Outside the Hall the winter wind swept through the streets of Cambridge. Inside all was warmth and conviviality. Along the tables a hundred candles ensconced in silver candelabra cast elongated shadows of the crouching waiters across the portraits of past Masters that lined the walls. Severe or genial, scholars or politicians, the portraits had one thing in common: they were all rubicund and plump. Porterhouse's kitchen was long established. Only the new Master differed from his predecessors. Seated at the High Table, Sir Godber Evans picked at his swan with a delicate hesitancy that was in marked contrast to the frank enjoyment of the Fellows. A fixed dyspeptic smile lent a grim animation to Sir Godber's pale features as if his mind found relief from the present discomforts of the flesh in some remote and wholly intellectual joke.

'An evening to remember, Master,' said the Senior Tutor sebaceously.

'Indeed, Senior Tutor, indeed,' murmured the Master, his private joke enhanced by this unsought prediction.

'This swan is excellent,' said the Dean. 'A fine bird and the widgeon gives it a certain *gamin* flavour.'

'So good of Her Majesty to give Her permission for us to have swan,' the Bursar said. 'It's a privilege very rarely granted, you know.'

'Very rare,' the Chaplain agreed.

'Indeed, Chaplain, indeed,' murmured the Master and crossed his knife and fork. 'I think I'll wait for the beefsteak.' He sat back and studied the faces of the Fellows with fresh distaste. They were, he thought once again, an atavistic lot, and never more so than now with their napkins tucked into their collars, an age-old tradition of the College, and their foreheads greasy with perspiration and their mouths interminably full. How little things had changed since his own days as an undergraduate in Porterhouse.

Tom Sharpe: *Porterhouse Blue*

Truffles

Rome, October 10, 1968

Dined last night with Etienne and Jane Burin des Roziers. He is now French ambassador here. He had a marvelous story about the French embassy in Washington when Henri Bonnet was Ambassador. Bonnet was giving an important dinner for Foster Dulles so he had truffles specially flown from France. When they arrived his chef brought them and Bonnet, sniffing them, thought they were too high. The chef assured him they were all right. 'Let's try them on the dog,' said Henri. They gave a chunk of truffle to his dog who enjoyed it.

The dinner went fine, truffles in the first course. When they were well along toward the cheese a pale butler brought Bonnet a brief note from the chef: 'The dog just died.' Henri blanched, excused himself, said he had an urgent telephone call. He called his doctor, asked his advice. How could he risk poisoning the secretary of state? The doctor said he would rush right over with emetic pills.

When Henri returned he suavely mentioned, as of little account, that sometimes people were sensitive to truffles. *En passant*, he added that his dog, who had shared this particular truffle, had just died so he had taken the precaution of obtaining some emetic pills. If any guest would feel safer he would be glad to provide a pill. All the guests, headed by Dulles, grabbed them. The various bathroom facilities were shared out among senior ranking guests and the ladies; the rest, including Bonnet, went out into the garden and retched.

Finally, after a disheveled, frantic group had reassembled and Bonnet was tranquilising them with cognac somebody asked: 'Did the dog suffer much? Did it take him long to die?' Bonnet thought this a good question and summoned the chef. Said the chef: 'Not at all, M. l'Ambassadeur. It was over in an instant. The truck hit him squarely and broke his neck.'

Cyrus Sulzberger: *An Age of Mediocrity*

The great eating contest

Maybe you hear something of this great eating contest that comes
off in New York one night in the early summer of 1937. Of course
eating contests are by no means anything new, and in fact they are
quite an old-fashioned pastime in some sections of this country, such
as the South and East, but this is the first big public contest of the
kind in years, and it creates no little comment along Broadway.

In fact, there is some mention of it in the blats, and it is not a
frivolous proposition in any respect, and more dough is wagered on
it than any other eating contest in history, with Joel Duffle a 6 to 5
favourite over Miss Violette Shumberger all the way through.

This Joel Duffle comes to New York several days before the contest
with the character by the name of Conway, and requests a meet with
Miss Violette Shumberger to agree on the final details and who shows
up with Miss Violette Shumberger as her coach and adviser but
Nicely-Nicely Jones. He is even thinner and more peaked-looking
than when Horsey and I see him last, but he says he feels great, and
that he is within six pounds of his marriage to Miss Hilda Slocum.

Well, it seems that his presence is really due to Miss Hilda Slocum
herself, because she says that after getting her dearest friend Miss
Violette Shumberger into this jackpot, it is only fair to do all she can
to help her win it, and the only way she can think of is to let
Nicely-Nicely give Violette the benefit of his experience and advice.

But afterward we learn that what really happens is that this editor,
Mr McBurgle, gets greatly interested in the contest, and when he
discovers that in spite of his influence, Miss Hilda Slocum declines
to permit Nicely-Nicely to personally compete, but puts in a pinch
eater, he is quite indignant and insists on her letting Nicely-Nicely
school Violette.

Furthermore we afterward learn that when Nicely-Nicely returns
to the apartment on Morningside Heights after giving Violette a
lesson, Miss Hilda Slocum always smells his breath to see if he
indulges in any food during his absence.

Well, this Joel Duffle is a tall character with stooped shoulders, and
a sad expression, and he does not look as if he can eat his way out of

a tea shoppe, but as soon as he commences to discuss the details of the contest, anybody can see that he knows what time it is in situations such as this. In fact, Nicely-Nicely says he can tell at once from the way Joel Duffle talks that he is a dangerous opponent, and he says while Miss Violette Shumberger impresses him as an improving eater, he is only sorry she does not have more seasoning.

This Joel Duffle suggests that the contest consist of twelve courses of strictly American food, each side to be allowed to pick six dishes, doing the picking in rotation, and specifying the weight and quantity of the course selected to any amount the contestant making the pick desires, and each course is to be divided for eating exactly in half, and after Miss Violette Shumberger and Nicely-Nicely whisper together a while, they say the terms are quite satisfactory.

Then Horsey tosses a coin for the first pick, and Joel Duffle says heads, and it is heads, and he chooses, as the first course, two quarts of ripe olives, twelve bunches of celery, and four pounds of shelled nuts, all this to be split fifty-fifty between them. Miss Violette Shumberger names twelve dozen cherry-stone clams as the second course, and Joel Duffle says two gallons of Philadelphia pepper-pot soup as the third.

Well, Miss Violette Shumberger and Nicely-Nicely whisper together again, and Violette puts in two five-pound striped bass, the heads and tails not to count in the eating, and Joel Duffle names a twenty-two pound roast turkey. Each vegetable is rated as one course, and Miss Violette Shumberger asks for twelve pounds of mashed potatoes with brown gravy. Joel Duffle says two dozen ears of corn on the cob, and Violette replies with two quarts of lima beans. Joel Duffle calls for twelve bunches of asparagus cooked in butter, and Violette mentions ten pounds of stewed new peas.

`This gets them down to the salad, and it is Joel Duffle's play, so he says six pounds of mixed green salad with vinegar and oil dressing, and now Miss Violette Shumberger has the final selection, which is the dessert. She says it is a pumpkin pie, two feet across, and not less than three inches deep.

It is agreed that they must eat with knife, fork or spoon, but speed is not to count, and there is to be no time limit, except they cannot pause more than two consecutive minutes at any stage, except in case of hiccoughs. They can drink anything, and as much as they please, but liquids are not to count in the scoring. The decision is to be strictly on the amount of food consumed, and the judges are to take account of anything left on the plates after a course, but not of loose chewings on bosom or vest up to an ounce. The losing side is to pay for the food, and in case of a tie they are to eat it off immediately on ham and eggs only.

Well, the scene of this contest is the second-floor dining-room of Mindy's restaurant, which is closed to the general public for the occasion, and only parties immediately concerned in the contest are admitted. The contestants are seated on either side of a big table in the centre of the room, and each contestant has three waiters.

No talking and no rooting from the spectators is permitted, but of course in any eating contest the principals may speak to each other if they wish, though smart eaters never wish to do this, as talking only wastes energy, and about all they ever say to each other is please pass the mustard.

About fifty characters from Boston are present to witness the contest, and the same number of citizens of New York are admitted, and among them is this editor, Mr McBurgle, and he is around asking Horsey if he thinks Miss Violette Shumberger is as good a thing as the jumper at the race track.

Nicely-Nicely arrives on the scene quite early, and his appearance is really most distressing to his old friends and admirers, as by this time he is shy so much weight that he is a pitiful scene, to be sure, but he tells Horsey and me that he thinks Miss Violette Shumberger has a good chance.

'Of course,' he says, 'she is green. She does not know how to pace herself in competition. But,' he says, 'she has a wonderful style. I love to watch her eat. She likes the same things I do in the days when I am eating. She is a wonderful character, too. Do you ever notice her smile?' Nicely-Nicely says.

'But,' he says, 'she is the dearest friend of my fiancée, Miss Hilda Slocum, so let us not speak of this. I try to get Hilda to come to see the contest, but she says it is repulsive. Well, anyway,' Nicely-Nicely says, 'I manage to borrow a few dibs, and am wagering on Miss Violette Shumberger. By the way,' he says, 'if you happen to think of it, notice her smile.'

Well, Nicely-Nicely takes a chair about ten feet behind Miss Violette Shumberger, which is as close as the judges will allow him, and he is warned by them that no coaching from the corners will be permitted, but of course Nicely-Nicely knows this rule as well as they do, and furthermore by this time his exertions seem to have left him without any more energy.

There are three judges, and they are all from neutral territory. One of these judges is a party from Baltimore, Md., by the name of Packard, who runs a restaurant, and another is a party from Providence, RI, by the name of Croppers, who is a sausage manufacturer. The third judge is an old Judy by the name of Mrs Rhubarb, who comes from Philadelphia, and once keeps an actors' boarding-house, and is considered an excellent judge of eaters.

Well, Mindy is the official starter, and at 8.30 p.m. sharp, when there is still much betting among the spectators, he outs with his watch, and says like this:

'Are you ready, Boston? Are you ready, New York?'

Miss Violette Shumberger and Joel Duffle both nod their heads, and Mindy says commence, and the contest is on, with Joel Duffle getting the jump at once on the celery and olives and nuts.

It is apparent that this Joel Duffle is one of these rough-and-tumble eaters that you can hear quite a distance off, especially on clams and soups. He is also an eyebrow eater, an eater whose eyebrows go up as high as the part in his hair as he eats, and this type of eater is undoubtedly very efficient.

In fact, the way Joel Duffle goes through the groceries down to the turkey causes the Broadway spectators some uneasiness, and they are whispering to each other that they only wish the old Nicely-Nicely is in there. But personally, I like the way Miss Violette Shumberger eats without undue excitement, and with great zest. She cannot keep close to Joel Duffle in the matter of speed in the early stages of the contest, as she seems to enjoy chewing her food, but I observe that as it goes along she pulls up on him, and I figure this is not because she is stepping up her pace, but because he is slowing down.

When the turkey finally comes on, and is split in two halves right down the middle, Miss Violette Shumberger looks greatly disappointed, and she speaks for the first time as follows:

'Why,' she says, 'where is the stuffing?'

Well, it seems that nobody mentions any stuffing for the turkey to the chef, so he does not make any stuffing, and Miss Violette Shumberger's disappointment is so plain to be seen that the confidence of the Boston characters is somewhat shaken. They can see that a

Judy who can pack away as much fodder as Miss Violette Shumberger has to date, and then beef for stuffing, is really quite an eater.

In fact, Joel Duffle looks quite startled when he observes Miss Violette Shumberger's disappointment, and he gazes at her with great respect as she disposes of her share of the turkey, and the mashed potatoes, and one thing and another in such a manner that she moves up on the pumpkin pie on dead even terms with him. In fact, there is little to choose between them at this point, although the judge from Baltimore is calling the attention of the other judges to a turkey leg that he claims Miss Violette Shumberger does not clean as neatly as Joel Duffle does his, but the other judges dismiss this as a technicality.

Then the waiters bring on the pumpkin pie, and it is without doubt quite a large pie, and in fact it is about the size of a manhole cover, and I can see that Joel Duffle is observing this pie with a strange expression on his face, although to tell the truth I do not care for the expression on Miss Violet Shumberger's face, either.

Well, the pie is cut in two dead centre, and one half is placed before Miss Violette Shumberger and the other half before Joel Duffle, and he does not take more than two bites before I see him loosen his waistband and take a big swig of water, and thinks I to myself, he is now down to a slow walk, and the pie will decide the whole heat, and I am only wishing I am able to wager a little more dough on Miss Violette Shumberger. But about this moment, and before she as much as touches her pie, all of a sudden Violette turns her head and motions to Nicely-Nicely to approach her, and as he approaches, she whispers in his ear.

Now at this, the Boston character by the name of Conway jumps up and claims a foul and several other Boston characters join him in this claim, and so does Joel Duffle, although afterwards even the Boston characters admit that Joel Duffle is no gentleman to make such a claim against a lady.

Well, there is some confusion over this, and the judges hold a conference, and they rule that there is certainly no foul in the actual eating that they can see, because Miss Violette Shumberger does not touch her pie so far.

But they say that whether it is a foul otherwise all depends on whether Miss Violette Shumberger is requesting advice on the contest from Nicely-Nicely and the judge from Providence, RI, wishes to know if Nicely-Nicely will kindly relate what passes between him and Violette so they may make a decision.

'Why,' Nicely-Nicely says, 'all she asks me is can I get her another piece of pie when she finishes the one in front of her.'

Now at this, Joel Duffle throws down his knife, and pushes back his plate with all but two bites of his pie left on it, and says to the Boston characters like this:

'Gentlemen,' he says, 'I am licked. I cannot eat another mouthful. You must admit I put up a game battle, but,' he says, 'it is useless for me to go on against this Judy who is asking for more pie before she even starts on what is before her. I am almost dying as it is, and I do not wish to destroy myself in a hopeless effort. Gentlemen,' he says, 'she is not human.'

Well, of course this amounts to throwing in the old napkin and Nicely-Nicely stands up on his chair, and says:

'Three cheers for Miss Violette Shumberger!'

Then Nicely-Nicely gives the first cheer in person, but the effort overtaxes his strength, and he falls off the chair in a faint just as Joel Duffle collapses under the table, and the doctors at the Clinic Hospital are greatly baffled to receive, from the same address at the same time, one patient who is suffering from undernourishment, and another patient who is unconscious from over-eating.

Well, in the meantime, after the excitement subsides, and wagers are settled, we take Miss Violette Shumberger to the main floor in Mindy's for a midnight snack, and when she speaks of her wonderful triumph, she is disposed to give much credit to Nicely-Nicely Jones.

'You see,' Violette says, 'what I really whisper to him is that I am a goner. I whisper to him that I cannot possibly take one bite of the pie if my life depends on it, and if he has any bets down to try and hedge them off as quickly as possible.

'I fear,' she says, 'that Nicely-Nicely will be greatly disappointed in my showing, but I have a confession to make to him when he gets out of the hospital. I forget about the contest,' Violette says, 'and eat my regular dinner of pig's knuckles and sauerkraut an hour before the contest starts and,' she says, 'I have no doubt this tends to affect my form somewhat. So,' she says, 'I owe everything to Nicely-Nicely's quick thinking.'

Damon Runyon: *A piece of pie*

Such a jolly meat pie

'He had better have something to eat, immediately,' remarked Emily.

The fat boy almost laughed again when he heard this suggestion. Mary, after a little more whispering, tripped forth from the group, and said:

'I am going to dine with you to-day, sir, if you have no objection.'

'This way,' said the fat boy, eagerly. 'There is such a jolly meat pie!'

With these words, the fat boy led the way down-stairs; his pretty companion captivating all the waiters and angering all the chamber-maids as she followed him to the eating-room.

There was the meat-pie of which the youth had spoken so feelingly, and there were, moreover, a steak, and a dish of potatoes, and a pot of porter.

'Sit down,' said the fat boy. 'Oh, my eye, how prime! I am *so* hungry.'

Having apostrophised his eye, in a species of rapture, five or six times, the youth took the head of the little table, and Mary seated herself at the bottom.

'Will you have some of this?' said the fat boy, plunging into the pie up to the very ferules of the knife and fork.

'A little, if you please,' replied Mary.

The fat boy assisted Mary to a little, and himself to a great deal, and was just going to begin eating when he suddenly laid down his knife and fork, leant forward in his chair, and letting his hands, with the knife and fork in them, fall on his knees, said, very slowly:

'I say! How nice you look!'

This was said in an admiring manner, and was, so far, gratifying; but still there was enough of the cannibal in the young gentleman's eyes to render the compliment a double one.

'Dear me, Joseph,' said Mary, affecting to blush, 'what do you mean?'

The fat boy gradually recovering his former position, replied with a heavy sigh, and remaining thoughtful for a few moments, drank a long draught of the porter. Having achieved this feat he sighed again, and applied himself assiduously to the pie.

'What a nice young lady Miss Emily is!' said Mary, after a long silence.

The fat boy had by this time finished the pie. He fixed his eyes on Mary, and replied:

'I knows a nicerer.'

'Indeed!' said Mary.

'Yes, indeed!' replied the fat boy, with unwonted vivacity.

'What's her name?' inquired Mary.

'What's yours?'

'Mary.'

'So's hers,' said the fat boy. 'You're her.' The boy grinned to add point to the compliment, and put his eyes into something between a squint and a cast, which there is reason to believe he intended for an ogle.

'You mustn't talk to me in that way,' said Mary; 'you don't mean it.'

'Don't I, though?' replied the fat boy; 'I say!'

'Well.'

'Are you going to come here regular?'

'No,' rejoined Mary, shaking her head, 'I'm going away again to-night. Why?'

'Oh!' said the fat boy in a tone of strong feeling; 'how we should have enjoyed ourselves at meals, if you had been!'

'I might come here sometimes, perhaps, to see you,' said Mary, plaiting the table-cloth in assumed coyness, 'if you would do me a favour.'

The fat boy looked from the pie-dish to the steak, as if he thought a favour must be in a manner connected with something to eat; and then took out one of the half-crowns and glanced at it nervously.

'Don't you understand me?' said Mary, looking slyly in his fat face.

Again he looked at the half-crown, and said faintly, 'No.'

'The ladies want you not to say anything to the old gentleman about the young gentleman having been upstairs; and I want you too.'

'Is that all?' said the fat boy, evidently very much relieved as he pocketed the half-crown again. 'Of course I ain't a going to.'

'You see,' said Mary, 'Mr Snodgrass is very fond of Miss Emily, and Miss Emily's very fond of him, and if you were to tell about it, the old gentleman would carry you all away miles into the country, where you'd see nobody.'

'No, no, I won't tell,' said the fat boy, stoutly.

'That's a dear,' said Mary. 'Now it's time I went upstairs, and got my lady ready for dinner.'

'Don't go yet,' urged the fat boy.

'I must,' replied Mary. 'Good bye, for the present.'

The fat boy, with elephantine playfulness, stretched out his arms to ravish a kiss; but as it required no great agility to elude him, his fair enslaver had vanished before he closed them again; upon which the apathetic youth ate a pound or so of steak with a sentimental countenance, and fell fast asleep.

Charles Dickens: *The Pickwick Papers*